495

Truth to Tell

GLENN CLAIRMONTE

Unity Books
Unity Village, Missouri 64065

Copyright © 1979 by Unity School of Christianity
Unity Village, Missouri 64065
Library of Congress Card Number: 78-66006

CONTENTS

Foreword / v
The History of You and Me / 9
The Loving Surrender / 19
The Inner Dialogue / 31
Shortcut to Perfection / 53
Putting It All Together / 65
Redeeming Memory / 85
Intuition to the Rescue / 99
The Long Reach of Telepathy / 115
The New Independence / 127
A Look at the Past / 139
Today's Evolution / 149
Each of Us a Self-Healer / 161
A Touch of Sublimity / 173
The Call of the Future / 185
How Wonderful We Are! / 197
The Marriage of Mind and Matter / 215
Are You in Love? If Not, Why Not? / 229
Humanity on the March / 245
What Is Your Intention? / 257
The Best Is Yet to Come / 269

Foreword

Since 1940, when her first Unity article appeared in *Good Business* Magazine, Glenn Clairmonte has contributed more than eighty articles to various Unity periodicals. Her writings have also appeared in numerous other magazines, journals, and newspapers. She is the author of two books: "Calamity Was the Name for Jane" and "John Sutter of California."

This volume is a compilation of articles which appeared in UNITY Magazine during the 1970s. The theme of this work and of its time is the expansion of self-awareness and the learning of human relatedness to the cosmos. Glenn Clairmonte is first and foremost an optimistic student of human nature. Stemming from this ardent interest is her work of writing, editing, researching, and lecturing about the latest trends in literature, religion, and science, with special focus on psychology and its sister, parapsychology.

Glenn Clairmonte takes pride in her human family. She traces the history of our growth in consciousness to the conclusion that we shall indeed evolve into even nobler human beings with increased appreciation for our environment and a grander sense of future direction. Mrs. Clairmonte teaches that each day brings us individually and collectively closer to the goal of true harmony and peace—within ourself, with each other, with the universe, and thus, with God.

It has been an honor to work with Glenn Clairmonte, and to have been on the receiving end of her magnificent ideas. I hope that each reader of this compilation will be imbued with those special qualities of vitality and joy that characterize Mrs. Clairmonte's work.

—*Janna Russell, Editor.*

Truth to Tell

The History of You and Me

Long ago, when natural conditions functioned to the point where a swerve was thrust out of matter, inorganic molecules jetted into living cells, thence to plants, to animals, and to human beings. Billions of atoms were pressing through their many channels, unknowingly magnetized toward the future which they had no eyes to see.

The cell division was followed by the organization of the molecules, which combined atoms, which in turn supplied radiant energy, accumulating all that had gone before and making a new contribution in the parade.

Let us for a moment envision how these capacities must have

become enlarged through level after level into bacteria and self-replicating sea creatures that in their turn were propelled to the land. Then that same silent and mysterious force, with its secret motive, produced insects and birds, and eventually mammals that have lasted for a mere split second of the unfathomable forever.

And here we are, trying to explain the transmission of nerve impulses that have brought us to what we are here and now.

No doubt at every change there was an expansion of calories by a quantum jump giving birth to another and another advance. During all those aeons, an inherent sense was traveling through many encumbrances toward the intimation and the final happening of consciousness. Thought itself was born out of incomprehension, and at last it knew that it knew. It has continued to extend itself until it has reached even the modern arousal of psychic recognition.

Believe it or not, we are finally able to look upon not only our past and our amazing present, but also upon our possible future. It has been a tedious and obscure trail before we could even suspect the growth of emotions, the beginning of sympathy, and other inner faculties. But the long delay is forgotten in the face of what has been accomplished in the matter of respect for others. This includes the warmth of admiration and even affection for other living things in their varying guises.

In a publication of UNICEF there is a photograph of a tiny child of the Middle East, an example of deprivation. He is hugging a baby goat's hooves against his chest in what is obviously a spasm of hunger for love. In its inarticulateness it looks to me like a token of human desire: all of us portrayed in this heartbreaking picture of what we want and dare not name.

We are unerringly moving toward the apex that is love, even though we are hardly able to define such a possibility.

The miracle of consciousness has changed the cell into a person who simply could not escape development, a person compelled to obey the same law that has provided all previous stages of growth. There is no possibility that we shall ever stop growing.

More and more noticeable is the important stage we are touching today—the general blending of mankind. Though we seem to be oblivious of the hidden purpose, we are constantly pressed toward a firmer feeling of the Presence that has always kept unfolding us during the swirl of the planets.

In merely being alive, we have been uninterruptedly moving toward a goal that is not only invisible, but also inconceivable, and above all, inevitable. At this particular moment, at last aware of the Supreme, we are forced to acknowledge that we are being impelled into a connection with the rest of humanity. Slowly all nations are learning to cooperate—sometimes against the will of their leaders—for it is becoming more and more apparent that only in one another's ambience shall we prosper.

Do you remember how once, through a microscope in the laboratory, we were observing the infinitesimal with wonder? Now we reluctantly encounter a larger view: the promise of unity of all aspects of life, the pressure toward closer and closer communication by the disparate nations. We can no longer ignore the value of the past, now that we have arrived at the present, and, though only grudgingly, we must submit to the encroachment of the future: the melding of peoples.

We are now impressed with the fact that space and time are only two human definitions of the one element in which we abide. This most recent step in our evolution is forcing us to associate with the very Power that heretofore worked through us without our recognition (much less our assistance).

Certainly all this has appeared out of what we called matter, though even that had a transcendence of its own. It is now proceeding in its usually uninterrupted manner into a mental acceptance that surprises us. We can no longer ignore that the cosmos is not only immense, not only durable, it is also alive and growing. Its already recognizable wonders are merely evidence of many more that we are only faintly beginning to notice. Until now, mere existence has seemed to be our fulfillment, and we have sailed about without even beginning to guess its possibilities. Yes, existence did support the bare outline of our experience, but now it prolongs our activity in a far more dazzling display.

Out of unseen roots we have grown beyond our former expectations. At last we realize that we are meant to survive even more astonishing changes. Especially, it is becoming clear that the forced march of livingness must be collective. Only by championing one another can all aspects of humanity fulfill the unimagined prophecy of the earliest cell. Only in a final unity can we incite the next and the next and the next rank. We are drawn by an eternally accomplished prediction, even while we are blind to the various destinations that still are predicted for us.

Our familiar equipment has provided enough incentive to permit of our former capacity, but now we are ready to produce a new era in which materialism and self-concern can no longer block the path. While we were unprepared for spirituality we had to manage without it, but as each new goal has attracted us, our consciousness has expanded, and we recognize that we are being unavoidably charmed toward the choice of unanimity.

This is the result of our having learned that an overall Presence contains us. We have been taking timid steps toward universal collaboration under that mystical governance, and now we are acquainted with a standard made realizable by our unexpected apprehension of superconsciousness. The result, whether we wisely appraise it or not, has revealed superhumanity as the next goal awaiting us. At last all segments of the world's population are awakening to the need to amalgamate.

How long, how long? It hardly matters, for the universal movement has never been judged by its rush, anyway.

Marcus Aurelius seems to have counted on the rightness of things when he trusted what he called "either gods or atoms." With what almost amounts to divine patience he declared: "All things are harmonious to me which are harmonious to thee, O Universe. Nothing for me is too early or too late which is in due time for thee."

He not only visualized the future unity of the races but he actually said, "We were made to work together, like feet, like hands, like eyelids, like the upper and lower teeth." And even further, "It is peculiar to man to love even those who do wrong; and thou wilt love them if, when they err, thou bethink thee that they are to thee near kin."

Certainly there is even less human impatience now that we realize how certain is our continual progress. Of course, we shall always be in flux, but the vision that all individuals are parts of a whole is giving us the claim of relationship. We are touched by the distant glow of love, and that adroit arousal of emotion is gradually supplying us with recognition that the earth itself is the essence of our nourishment. Already we human beings are yearning for a larger horizon than that which has so far encompassed us. Therefore, we consider matter and spirit as partners, seeing how the former has been molding us toward the disclosure of the other.

What Gopi Krishna has called "the inexorable pressure of evolutionary processes" now reveals itself internationally, in the political meetings that some people look upon as a kind of gentleman's war. When our impulses have established harmony in our environment and when the anger of self-interest has been reduced, the tendency toward covetousness will be overcome by an intellectual approach.

Richard Bach has said, "What a caterpillar calls the end of the world the Master calls a butterfly," and, indeed, out of the cocoon of the past these international assemblages are gradually supplying a whole new phase of collaboration.

Truth to tell, some of the most variable peoples are drawing together to discuss by imperceptible degrees the elimination of dissensions, the amelioration of contrasts, the reduction of distinguishing characteristics that have resulted from geographical separations. All of us are mingling our formerly colliding goals and combining for the magic of a successful conclusion, the ideal of a fully related humanity.

Beyond that we do not need to foresee, but when we analyze the history of you and me, we are gratified to admit how surely we are on the way.

William James once reminded us that "Every image has in itself a motor element," and the present-day possibility of world cooperation carries within it the blessing of a truly developed civilization. Every neighborly exchange in every small village is helping to build the ideal world community that the whole race of man shall enjoy under the divine plan that we now know exists.

Take heart! The higher control has always been for the better, and each age has always disclosed a finer achievement.

The Loving Surrender

The melody of "Shall We Dance, Shall We Dance" is ringing through my thoughts as I begin to write on the subject of meditation. This is because the dream, forerunner of meditation, means invasion of the upper air, as dance does too. To dance is to lift the limbs and undulate; to dream is to float into the chimerical realm for the sake of insight's deepening.

Even as music encourages the dance, so does surrender of the body to the effortless swing of the mind invite a fingertip touch upon the next highest goal. The virtue of all living things is "continual concern with the future," as Edmund Sinnott, the botanist, discovered.

A child sits erect in a hammock and lets one toe push against the earth at intervals to keep the sway. Eyes glazed, he silently coaches the imagination, "Wander where you will." And all the conjured pictures are about what may yet come to pass.

The child in each of us in secret moments trains upon such a private dreaming and thus fertilizes the vines whose tendrils reach and reach and reach with endless ardor. This is a rich undertaking, more productive of growth than is usually guessed.

Every life is colored by the presence of goals that have been elected unconsciously during such leisurely reveries. Random thoughts coalesce into a wish, and subsequent action proceeds from the conviction that this wish can be made manifest. A wish is not so cool as reason; rather, it is passionate and demanding. It is justified by its intensity, for it comprises delight, even reverence, and it drives toward a climax, often erecting its own culmination.

When the Kerley family heard of a country place that was for sale, they drove out of the city and through the seductive hills toward the designated address. They found a pretty house covered with crimson ramblers, and surrounding it there were ten acres of wild flowers in bloom. Because of the distance from Mr. Kerley's daily appointments, as well as because of the expense, it seemed unwise for them to make the purchase.

But Chris Kerley, the youngest member of the family, sensing something more exacting than the obvious, challenged the others, "If we can't have it, then why did we ever see it?"

Mr. and Mrs. Kerley looked at each other with the unspoken question: Can we? Shall we?

And the decision was made to settle there and to meet difficulties as they should arise. The clarity of the child's wish won its proper future.

One of Chris' older sisters whispered to him, "You're smart!" and he seemed puzzled as to why she had said this.

An observer may be surprised that such resultant behavior despite financial considerations shows better judgment than former tendencies might have done. The craving for promotion seems so fundamentally right that any blockage gives the impression of injury, and to take the venture means moving toward something more than physical indulgence. Of course the evidence varies with the individual, with the time, and with the location as well as with other circumstances. It may seem to be the wave of instinctive longing, but it does more than stir emotion: it aims at a gradually revealed intention. In one range such a feeling amounts to awe, while the activity confirms a connection between the self and the destination, between the pulse of the organism and the environment.

Sinnott continues: "The self is the essence of man's aspirations.... It is not a static, nebulous, ghostly thing but a search and a desiring; a pattern in living stuff which seeks to be fulfilled.... We do what we will to do."

As the embryo arranges matter into a pattern, and as the pattern regulates adulthood through instinct, there is interminably an orderly purposiveness, a persistent relationship between spirit and matter which begins to operate during the initial processes of protoplasm. Therefore you can see it is a mistake to imply that spirit may be separate from body equipment. For instance, the contraries of courage and shame have their place in both aspects, formulating the body-plus-spirit, the two parts being complementary because one without the other is inconceivable. Without the material, what could be created? Without the creative, what could reside in the material?

Precious human traits like curiosity and sympathy are still unexplained, but we want to define them in order to savor them fully, in order to expand their essence. Are we confounded to postulate that such qualities may have had their germ in matter? If spirit is that which pervades the universe and from which all life emerges, then physical attributes too must be seen as belonging to that universe. Perhaps it is the fusion that constructs our ideals, exemplifying the Divine in the blend.

Each of the alluring goals, from earliest to loftiest, begins in a wish. In one step after another each rises in value through the centuries, always predicting still new values to come. Each goal in its turn is transcended, each is used as a toehold so that another may be attained. Refinement of desire tantalizes with each succession.

Our search for beauty and righteousness makes us ask, "How does spirit function within the flesh?" By the leap of intuition (religious fervor)? Nature supplies the answer by joining emotion with substance.

We don't know by what means living substance recognizes the importance of goals, but aspire we do, gathering up our incessantly transforming consciousness—in fact, meditating.

Sir George Trevelyan says that meditation is "the art and practice of creating an inner centre of quiet and stillness within the self and then allowing this to be flooded with light from higher planes."

First we must realize that meditation is not subject to determination but can be accomplished only by the lessening of weight when the ego is allowed to drop away. Let go of self-interest—let it go! Although we are glad to acknowledge the truth of our individual worth, no single one of us can believe himself indispensable (the world lives even without Plato and Michelangelo and Galileo). See yourself as one in the great parade of cheerers-on, then be lost in admiration of the brightly shining Whole.

Be willing to learn what has never been known before, and thus travel inward. To leave here and arrive somewhere else means not only starting, but also achieving an end. This presupposes a purpose.

The Lama Govinda claims that "our mind, unless it is channeled in a predetermined direction, begins to move here and there and, by merely observing the meandering flow of our thoughts and emotions and mental images, we may get a certain insight into the functions of consciousness, but nothing more."

Consequently he praises one who can contemplate "the perfect representation of the spiritualized man who, without losing the solid ground of reality beneath his feet, accepting and ennobling his corporeality . . . is at peace with himself and with the world."

The objective must be tranquillity and independence of external things — in other words, self-completion.

Realize that meditation cannot be hastened any more than the opening of the dawn can be. Only when you have long entertained the background thoughts that establish a spiritual climate can you consciously advance, as it is natural for all living organisms to do, each upon its own level. The life process includes response to a universal drawing power.

This is what is called motivation — a realization of the initiative taken by an irresistible force whose pursuit enfolds you. Magnetized by the yet-to-be-gained, in wonder and joy you know that the hunger of spirit is about to be gratified.

Even without estimating the character of the Ultimate, you are enticed further and further into the interior enlightenment. Words and actions are forgotten, for meditation's first intimation is the stillness that is its own reward.

When first you sit at ease and suppress the little nervous reactions of the body, if you hear a dog's bark, if you become aware of street noises outside your window, if a faucet is dripping, bless them as part of the Whole surrounding you. Then forget them as you make your separate way into the quiet place where you have decided to abide.

If you are tempted to fret because vagrant images of former worries besiege you—

"If I'd only known then—"

"I wish I'd made restitution—"

"I should never have been so rude—"

accept these as symptoms of a receding past and declare them redeemed. Let a poised mind move unresistingly beyond them, while your emotions and your intellect interlock.

Hold to the "mindfulness of breathing and allow all else to follow at its own pace." When you are attached to your personal center of gravity you become aware of your breathing, that body motion normally outside of your control. But now it seems proper for you to follow its rhythm of inhalation and exhalation. So you are on the way to immersion in the oneness of the universe.

Gradually you approach the field where feeling and thinking are together resident. Next, you drift past them to the indescribable concord that creates "a chamber of silence in the heart." You experience spontaneous union of all the currents of your humanness and see your complex truth that has always existed though it has not been recognized.

"As our thoughts dwell on something beautiful and significant," says Helen Newman, "a creative action is begun."

Here at last you are truly meditating, knowing the compensation for your invested devotion.

The foundation of this enterprise is your personal acceptance of spiritual guidance. No other person's advice will have importance for you when you have learned for yourself what the combination is.

Mrs. Elkins told me that, after she forgot the things around her and the things she had to do tomorrow, she halted in a column of cool, sweet air. Then came a realization that was a reversal of her earlier inference.

"When I was all that quiet," she said, "it became clear to me that I ought never to have acted like a child, deciding what I wanted and demanding it of God. It's much better for me to receive the Father's loving gift. With His perspective He knows far more than I do about the things that are good for me. How strange that I never knew that before. Besides, what He wants us to have is always right there for us."

Another friend whom I call Sparky was still in a state of surprise when he said, "I came out of what I suppose you would call a meditation, and I scarcely moved for a moment. It was almost as if I didn't want to move and didn't have to. And the first thing I noticed as I looked out of the window was an apricot tree flooded with blossoms. The funny thing about it was that it was the season when that tree never has anything but bare boughs."

Evidently a sense of the future had overtaken Sparky.

There is no way of telling what my other

friends will experience upon arriving at the moment when they too feel the need to look deeply into themselves.

Shall we dream? That is, shall we meditate? Just try to stop us! For this we were born.

The Inner Dialogue

Naturalist Les Blacklock has confided that one day he sought advice at the "therapist's couch," a moss-covered log slowly sifting its values back into the earth from where they had long ago emerged: "Surrounded by the serene wisdom of nature my problems seem more manageable. In this uncluttered bit of time it has been possible to see my day-to-day life in new perspective. I get up and stroll away, mind and body refreshed."

Millions of us have had a similar experience when we reverted to the natural, for only subconsciously, it seems, can our mind acquire respite from the intellect. The secret soliloquy permits the private self to behold its dearest dream.

Early in this century psychology was sometimes called the youngest of the sciences, but many considered such a claim presumptuous until a group of scientists accepted it as one of their disciplines. Its successor, parapsychology, was a stepchild until it first won the sanction of the American Association for the Advancement of Science.

Until recently there was only scattered recognition that the human reaction known as religion could be assumed as belonging within the technique of psychology, despite William James' bold gestures in that direction. His "Varieties of Religious Experience" (1902) leaned heavily upon mental activity, and it is still widely read.

There have been many changes in scholarly areas—all gradual, to be sure, for trained minds are too proud to make precipitate leaps. The "mod" thing is to combine the various personality traits and concepts of the whole human range. For this reason we are prepared to understand Les Blacklock's pause in the forest, and even a city man may find renewal by delving into his psyche.

Rennie Riker decided to experiment with the kind of inner dialogue he had read about but had never credited. Needing capital to expand his business and having discussed the matter with his sweetheart, he was touched by her suggestion. She said: "Don't look to anyone else for advice. The whole idea of your work originated with you, didn't it? Then inside of you is the only advice you need."

Carol represented such warmth and faith and beauty and tenderness that he could not readily dismiss her diagnosis. Although he knew he had not the financial finesse to impress the average investor, he hoped she was in touch with a truth that had so far eluded him. Therefore he walked slowly through the downtown section of a big city, eyes straight ahead as he ignored the crowd swirling around him. He was trying to find the advice within him that Carol believed in.

Before long the name *Crandall* appeared in Riker's thoughts, and he caught at it as though it were a bird that must not be allowed to escape. *Crandall, Crandall, Crandall,* he let his mind roll over. Absentmindedly he turned into the building where he banked — and there the name *Crandall* fell into its right niche, for he had seen that name on a plate upon one of the polished desks at the right of the bank lobby. He looked for that name now, and slowly but not hesitantly he approached it.

"Mr. Crandall?" he inquired when the man behind the desk looked up to greet him.

"Mr. Crandall is on vacation, but perhaps I can be of help," the young bank officer replied.

Indeed he could and did help. He listened to Riker's plan and questioned him informatively, then made arrangements to approve a loan. In subsequent dealings with that bank, Riker learned that Crandall would never have backed him. The vacation replacement at Crandall's desk was the man with the special experience to show faith in Riker's scheme.

When Carol asked breathlessly, "Rennie, how did it go?" he answered, "It was so easily done that if I'd had time to think it over I might have said it was impossible. But after getting that answer inside my head, I knew I was being led."

It used to be the custom to consider an episode like this as part of the mystery called religion and, just as religion as a subject for scientific study was long denied, intuition too has been patronized as anything but dependable. But today's reliable psychologists are recommending the cultivation of intuition. They outline methods by which hidden truths may be enticed into the open by symbolism that can be traced through history back to primitive man.

Dr. Roberto Assagioli was not alone in pressing for what he called psychosynthesis. Painstakingly he portrayed the "spiritual Self" as the guide to be trusted for counsel in crisis, even praised its authority. This shows that scientists and mystics have been coalescing of late. Fortunately neither Les Blacklock nor Rennie Riker had waited for psychology's approval before proceeding with his own inner dialogue.

Despite records left by Thomas Aquinas

and Jacob Boehme and the saints, nobody who claimed to be practical gave credence to the silent prayer that was in earlier eras the journey to the unconscious or superconscious. Its lack of acceptance may have been due to the absence of a jargon that could win public approval. There is certainly nothing difficult in this arduously constructed maxim found in Dr. Assagioli's work:

> Sometimes the answer is delayed and comes in an unexpected moment, when the personality is not looking for it and is perhaps occupied with other concerns.

In precisely these words many of us have been saying this for years and being snubbed as visionaries.

Interminably, advocates of intuition have counseled a "letting go" to facilitate the reception of the "message." Interminably also they have explained that "tenseness can constitute an obstacle to receptivity." Now the nay-sayers, forgetting their long resistance, have made their own announcement in their own word combinations to describe intuitive impressions as related to the entire package of a person's life within his unique environment:

> Sometimes the answer comes seemingly spontaneously through a third person or through a book or other reading material, or through the development of circumstances themselves.

This agrees with numerous reports that a random shuffling of pages (often in the Bible, if that turned out to be the only book at hand) has given direction to save a life or a fortune. Nowadays the casual turning of a radio dial has elicited pertinent information, or a television character has blurted out a line that the listener has followed to a fortunate conclusion.

"This should not surprise us too much," says the psychologist, and he adds that perhaps such enlightenment is always available though unrecognized, that heretofore it has been repressed only by bigotry.

> But the fact of formulating a question and being in a state of general expectation helps us to register and recognize what would otherwise remain hidden.

Yes, of course. Why else has prayer, so well delineated in that sentence, been frequently recommended to one facing a dilemma? There could be no better explanation of our reason for resorting to listening by a more invisible organ than the ear. How else have people in every land during every age known the relationship between the one who prays and his satisfaction?

If you have ever made a prayer, you have already used the extrasensory perception that so many people are talking about these days. Prayer is the arrow shot beyond time and space, your only tool for exerting personal control over a situation.

Primitive man, before he had any language for expressing his thoughts, knew instinctively that he wanted to reach a higher rung. That deep purpose of life, growth, was working in him as it has been working in all living things, from the first single cell that started the parade up through all forms of life, even into the highly sophisticated person that you are. The purpose constantly shows itself, and we yearn because it is our nature to yearn.

Growth is happiness, and yearning is one stage of that growth.

Long before there were words to reflect that yearning, what we now call prayer came about. When primitive man prayed without words, that was the first time a human being shot an arrow beyond time and space and so contacted the benefits he hungered for. Ever since then, all of us have been following his example. There is no law that says you cannot do the same.

The universe asks only, "Do you really mean it?" If you can sincerely reply, "Yes, yes!" the connection is made. If you hesitate and murmur, "Well, maybe," that doubt cancels the prayer and things continue to be as they were before you made it.

The logic of the universe protects you from making a mistake. For instance, when you pray for a certain thing you are convinced that it entails happiness. Now, if that object is not guaranteed to bring you happiness, it is bypassed and happiness comes by another route in conformance with your original intention. The words you use do not have as much importance as your true wish. Even plants, those early examples of life, react to their gardener's thoughts and not to his words. As a delicate part of the system, they confirm the something strangely clever about that system.

After your body and your mind have their full growth from childhood to adulthood, your spirit continues to grow in the learning that gradually leads to civilization. If, because of a childish whim, you think you deserve something better than someone else deserves, you will learn the necessary lesson by the backlash of your wrong thoughts. If you are careless enough to make a prayer that is meant to harm someone else, that harm backs up on you. As Emerson says, if you plant the peas in a crooked row, they come up just as you planted them.

Now and then you will reach a point where you feel forced to stop and listen. Your thoughts take on a quiet new direction: a willingness to face the deepest honesty inside you. That is the best proof that you have been growing.

Mrs. Snyder was playing the hose on her rose garden when the ringing of the telephone summoned her indoors. After her conversation with a distant friend she looked for her watch, and it was not on her wrist. She seated herself and became still, ankles and elbows resting, brain at the waiting pose. She said quietly, "Where did I leave that watch?" The reply came into her mind: In the pocket of your apron after you washed the breakfast dishes. This was not the first time she had enjoyed that sort of inner dialogue, so she rose at once.

In the kitchen the apron was hanging on the back of the pantry door, and of course the watch lay safely in one pocket.

At last we dare to count on intuition which is (as Jung said) not dependent upon reason but outside the province of reason. On its own level, intuition is free of personal wish and discloses a reality that the mind cannot refute.

The value of intuition lies in the way it provides information that is usually kept latent. In a pressing situation, it replaces helplessness. Of course it is rare, and some individuals have failed to differentiate a sentimental generalization from a genuine revelation. For this reason intuition has been discounted, just as fraud has robbed other fields of respect. (But G.K. Chesterton reminded us that the passing of a counterfeit bank note is no sign that the Bank of England does not exist—rather, to the contrary.)

"Anyone who is intuitive, who spontaneously and naturally uses the intuition," Assagioli continues, "experiences what it is without any need of explanation or demonstration."

Yes again. We know that a direct comprehension devoid of emotion can be activated by focus, but it must have appreciation before its benefit can be felt.

Sometimes intuition has been looked upon as a special dispensation for certain privileged individuals. On the other hand, often it has been urged that anyone can sample it after first "cleansing the consciousness" so as to supply empathy enough to accept a surprise. But its essence can be laid aside as extraneous unless the will is trained to exclude distractions and retain the fleeting thought.

Nell Graham has been a housewife for several years, but when it was important for her to earn money she went to the nearest city in order to look for a job. She was not exactly sure how to proceed. Vaguely she hoped to find an employment agency and begin at that point. But when she walked into one big office building that she had seen long ago, she recalled that a certain man with headquarters in this building had praised her work. It seemed that if only she could locate him today, he might prove to be a helpful connection. But what was his name? What company did he represent? She could not remember.

There was no use consulting the huge directory in the lobby, but she stood beside that wall and made an effort to empty her mind. She had to still the emotion that memory of the old acquaintance had aroused. It was a simple matter to ignore the people rushing to and fro and the cries of the elevator starter. She remained as though waiting for someone; in fact she was waiting for something. Abruptly the name *Rosenquist* emerged from her subconscious, and she found it on the directory in its proper alphabetical spot.

When she walked into his office on the fortieth floor, Mr. Rosenquist greeted her by saying: "What luck, Mrs. Graham, that you should have stopped in today! I was thinking of you this morning, because you're the only one I've met who has the training for a certain job that I have to fill. Are you free to take it?"

Mr. Rosenquist thought that Nell Graham's call was in answer to his need, and she thought it was in answer to hers. Arthur Koestler would explain that it was one of the important uncoincidental coincidences. A few years ago it would have been considered magic, or else an episode falsely reported.

Intuitive perception follows the relaxation of muscular and nervous tension, the freeing of the brain from unrelated matters and from personal bias. When the subconscious takes over, the result comes gently, offering no pressure, sustaining no doubt.

Some instances of intuition, or even examples of mind reading, have been tagged psychic when the information divulged seemed to be "messages from those we call dead." At other times they have been interpreted as supernormal because they implied unusual perspective as well as creative talent. But veridical intuition contains telepathy as well as precognition. In our misinterpretation we have been inserting a sense of mystery where it does not belong.

There were two sisters named Veronica and Lois, who continually disturbed each other although they were too polite to say so. Neither could say anything without hearing the same thing echoed in the words of the other. As children, when they were at lunch side by side, they used the same rhythm for raising the spoon of soup to the mouth. When one of them changed for the sake of variety, the other immediately changed also, as though whatever her sister did must be the proper way to act. Neighbors noticed their lockstep before Veronica and Lois did.

When they went to buy clothes they both chose the same style and the same color and did not dare accuse each other of imitation. Neither had the courage to change her mind and retreat to another choice. The result was that they were soon bored at seeing themselves duplicated. As they grew older and were able to live apart, there were still similarities that annoyed them. Their mailed Christmas gifts to each other turned out not to be an assuagement but an annoyance. One summer while on a trip in a far corner of the country, Veronica called on old friends. Out of politeness she refrained from reporting to Lois on the ill will she encountered, not believing that Lois would ever arrive in that far place. But a short time later Lois made a point of doing as her sister had done and made a similar call. This was disastrous, for it agitated the matter beyond good sense.

Their mutual embarrassment was prolonged. They had never been alike in temperament, only in behavior, and their exasperation increased while they persisted in remaining in conventional touch.

One day Veronica decided she could no longer endure the undefined rough edge between them, and she decided to reach for a solution. Having no prayer pillow, she knelt on a thick rug beside her bed, elbows on a pile of pillows, face in her palms, and threw the problem out into the higher dimension.

She said to herself, "I won't get up from here until I learn how to get rid of the irritation between us."

She silently listened with her inner ears and with her heart as well. She had tried this before and had usually been impatient, hurrying away before she noticed any response. But this time she was prepared to wait all day. She guessed there must be harmony to be found if only she could get the "right combination," as she phrased it.

Scarcely half an hour had elapsed when suddenly Veronica was aware of a curious kind of pleasure. An unexpected willingness to "let go" burned like a flame throughout her body. Against the will of the unhappy child she had formerly been, she surrendered to her sister. It was a surprise, because she had never suspected that surrender was necessary.

In that moment she knew that everything was loving between Lois and herself. She rose and went about her duties with renewed vitality and a smile on her lips. It seemed that until now she had never loved herself, much less her sister. At last she loved both of them, and the wave that joined them was refreshing and delightful.

The greatest happiness known is the feeling of love for others. When we love we are realizing our oneness with others, and this comfort is surpassing sweetness. It is said that first we have to love ourself, to know that we are okay (in today's psychological code). Next we must realize that others too are okay. Naturally others reflect our thoughts and react: if we are smart enough to see how good they are, we must be nice. In that exchange of admiration each of us becomes a dynamo, and the spark of pleasure dances between us.

Veronica had expected to be "told" in the

silence that there was something she ought to do, but it turned out that there was nothing to be done inasmuch as love had flooded over everything else.

During that day Mrs. Sullivan, a neighbor who was having unhappy relations with her daughter-in-law, came to confide in Veronica, and because Veronica was still beaming from her morning's deep experience, she described it to her caller.

Mrs. Sullivan asked anxiously, "Now what do you have to do?"

"Nothing," Veronica answered triumphantly. "It has already been done. All I have to do is send love to my sister whenever I think of her."

"But," Mrs. Sullivan remonstrated, "there must be something you ought to do. I'm willing to do anything to please my daughter-in-law, but everything I do seems to make her dislike me more."

"There's nothing to do but love," Veronica repeated, still at the height of her revelation.

As she said this it occurred to her that part of Mrs. Sullivan's trouble was that she was always *doing* something, as she herself and Lois had been *doing,* omitting love from their relationship. Now she had subtracted herself from the situation, and that seemed to make all the difference. She tried to make Mrs. Sullivan understand this, but she realized that was more *doing.* She had to stop, and surround Mrs. Sullivan with love. For some of us it is very difficult to stop *doing* and love instead. We seem not to realize that love is a force as steady as gravitation, negated only by obstacles that we place in its way.

A few days later Lois crossed the country and paid Veronica a surprise visit. Whether or not Veronica's love had drawn her (love has a way of doing that), whether or not she herself had achieved her own release from the unreasonable rivalry, they came together in their first mutual adult contact. Both cared for their news, both rejoiced in each other's separate successes. Neither had ever met anyone more to be admired, and in their delivery from a compulsion to match, they were now ready to acknowledge this admiration.

The former restraint remained only in the fact that neither confessed having sought the inner dialogue. Partially they were still too shy, partially they were so well imbued with the new happiness that words could be suspended.

Assuredly the inner dialogue can go far to enhance life, and it deserves to be explored by every one of us. At any time of stress, let us take a deep breath and recall the ancient advice, "With all your getting, get understanding." It is the original and the final resource.

Shortcut to Perfection

Often in my reading I find language that is felicitous enough to draw tears to my eyes, in humility for my own less melodious phrases. But almost never do I ponder, "Wish I'd said that!"

However, there is one certain sublime exclamation that could have made me everlastingly proud if I might have said it first. These are the words reported to have been spoken by Jesus under stress, "Father, forgive them; for they know not what they do."

Such a short appeal must have sounded breathless. Only in the depth of illumination could He have understood so clearly the abyss of unawareness in which His tormentors operated. Only the height of love could have caused Him to desire to protect them from the consequences of their act—to beseech God to "remember not their sins." It is an example of spontaneous and complete self-forgetfulness.

"Ignorance of the law is no excuse" was not in His vocabulary. He excused His attackers especially because of their ignorance. In comparison with the vengeful resentment that some of His supposed followers perpetrated upon their own opposition in succeeding centuries, His exaltation at that moment is beyond estimation.

When Albert Schweitzer and others were investigating the archives for information about "the historical Jesus," someone said, "If there never was such a Person, then whoever invented Him must have been equally distinguished, for no ordinary soul could have contrived that kind of fiction."

One fact that shows the simple refinement of the story as all the more remarkable is that it occurred in the era when the Roman soldiers were in occupation, when the temple priests were jealous of the rights they had fought to retain, and when the governor representing Caesar had to avoid a public riot if he did not wish to be recalled to Rome in disgrace. In that context it was certainly unusual that anyone at all should ever have preached with such humble poise—and should have culminated His career with that unasked-for pardon.

Some of us have been acquainted with Christians who make a constant effort to conduct their lives according to Jesus' pattern, pausing at intervals to demand of themselves, "Did I give the advice that Jesus would have given?" or "Have I sent out any uncharitable thoughts this day?" or "Was there something I neglected to do today that Jesus would have done?"

It would be hard to fault such a practice, and many of us diligently read books and magazines which suggest a discipline that will (we hope) lead us along a comparable path. We are often exhorted to analyze our motives and to judge our speech and action with the intention of consciously directing them every hour of every day. It is true that unrelenting attention is essential if we are to exercise our inner quality, as an athlete exercises his muscles. We can empathize with Alfred Tennyson who said: "There are moments when I feel and know the flesh to be the vision, God and the spiritual the only real and true. Depend upon it, the spiritual is real."

In correcting undesirable habits we see that the obstacles we encounter are part of the training, as hurdles at a track meet have their just position. Every difficulty we meet is a problem to be solved. Nothing we find "in our way" is there by accident, nor by mistake, you may be sure. It has arrived only when required by what we are, to help press us onward. If we try to circumvent it or mitigate its influence, our progress is merely postponed. The same problem will pop up again, perhaps at a less propitious hour. Any deterrent is matched by some reluctant interior impulse, but when that impulse has been transcended the trend toward betterment fortifies the outer motion so that it becomes properly modulated. We hasten our growth only by amending the traits of character that have led to discord. Naturally, the reason such correction is demanded is that we are less than divine; knowing that, we long for the profit of change.

There is only one shortcut to perfection, one sure method of avoiding detours: that is the cultivation of love, and we delay because too many times we follow a circuitous route toward that.

Lisette, being plain and wishing for love, decided to seek beauty on a pilgrimage from shrine to shrine.

At a certain wayside niche a young man told her, "To have beauty you must wear the cross of St. Julian."

"And where may I find the cross of St. Julian?" Lisette inquired, looking past his shoulder to the road that led to another shrine.

"Here," said the young man. "This is the cross of St. Julian."

He placed a kiss on Lisette's lips; whereupon Lisette grew radiant with the very beauty she had been seeking in her pilgrimage.

In gratitude Lisette returned home and carried gifts to the altar of the village church. But there the bent old priest looked reproachfully upon her.

"In truth, Lisette," the graybeard said reproachfully, "you are as plain as ever you were. Surely you have been deceived. More's the pity that you did not complete your pilgrimage."

Lisette was downcast but unshaken in her determination to be worthy of love. She set out once more and traveled from shrine to shrine, saying her tranquil prayers.

When again she had come to make her devotions in the sacred spot where the young man had spoken to her, her faith in the miracle was revived at sight of him.

"Truly, was I deceived?" she asked him hopefully.

He smiled into her puzzled face.

"I forgot to tell you," the young man said, "that the cross of St. Julian must be renewed every day, else the beauty it brings may vanish."

"Then I shall never leave you," Lisette told him, placing her lips before his and waiting for him to apply the cross of St. Julian again.

He did so, gently.

Presently he asked her, "Why did you set out to pray for beauty, when it was love you wanted?"

"I thought that only with beauty would it be possible to find love."

Then he answered: "Love comes first, with all other good things in its train. See, my little friend—now that you have found love, beauty has been added also."

How many of us seek mistakenly? How many of us ask for what we want without knowing that we must give the same to others?

Actually love is a substance that we can generate within ourself, and we ought continuously to be broadcasting it in all directions. But such a custom we can hardly accomplish "except by prayer and fasting."

In this case the prayer must be a conjunction with the dimension beyond self-bias, and the fasting must be the exclusion of all tendencies toward cruelty in any slight degree. Success in such an endeavor develops a sensitivity to intuition, and when the heart-feeling is based on integrity of purpose, this intuition provides the delicate instruction that makes each step of the ladder easier of access.

To give oneself to the grand aspiration means to realize that all sorrows and all triumphs are uniformly enlightening, all experiences unfolding more and more of life's scope. While you move toward the summit, you hear music that quickens the march. Your perspective enlarges, your passions ameliorate, your mind achieves a firmer control over emotions, until at last you are free of fear, worry, greed, and all the other so-called human characteristics that have caused injury to yourself and others. Wave on wave of warmth issues from you. You see its result upon flowers and children as you pass them, for love replaces the old personal poisons that your attitudes once manufactured without your knowing it.

Of course your aim expands as your ideals crystallize; your faults turn into talents; the brain is stimulated to sturdier effect. You drop from your shoulders the weight of possessiveness, and every job you do reflects a superior value. As your inclinations become well balanced, you use moderation even in your search for holiness. There is no haste because eternity is now; there is no temptation because all things are yours already. There is no tension, because there is no competition. There is plenty for all, and nobody has to hurry to get his share.

While you are engaged in this private project, automatically you distill an essence of devotion that perfumes your surroundings. There are many like you functioning in a similar range, enhancing their own vitality as they alter the rhythm of their living, and thus environment produces a new species.

No doubt you have noticed signs that thousands of our contemporaries are practicing the art of contemplation in a longing for the fruit of the Absolute. The "flower children" were not the first ones; the "make-love-not-war" advocates are not the last. Almost all of us are trying to rebuild character as we search for a symbolic form of religious fervor that fulfills the artistic requirement, the harbinger of a granting of the spirit's desire.

These forces are interacting and interpenetrating. Transcendence is inherent in humanity and must find its expression beyond the ascetic or the sacramental satisfactions of earlier centuries. Today's urgent unrest is a natural phenomenon that has always been confronted, as it has always been suspect by those who have forgotten their own age of meeting challenges. How otherwise than by the phalanx of youth could mankind have charged this far ahead? Said Rabindranath Tagore: "Life must increasingly outgrow its dwelling place. Man is immortal; therefore he must die endlessly. For life is a creative idea; it can find itself only in changing forms."

Vera Stanley Alder has made this comment about human beings: "The strange thing is that they consider themselves important; each minute one of them is able to feel that he is more important than the whole universe upon which he is but a speck." And she assures us, "Within man's tiny personality there is locked a power which will give him unlimited understanding of things quite beyond his physical reach, a dynamic capacity to wield the forces of Nature with a mind of which he knows not the limits."

An Authority above the known order is energizing humanity in the exploration of possibilities, and it is inevitable that every forward move should release a current to sweep the masses along toward surpassing experiences. At this time even the scholastic atmosphere is peculiarly favorable for the outcropping of man's dormant mystic faculty. We are daring to let our innate psychic sparks inflame the long-stifled instinct for eternity. We are able at last to deliver love for all living creatures and even for plants of the land and the sea. We are truly becoming a "new race" with a core of love that may still learn to communicate in the way we have observed in the story of Jesus.

This brings us back to the sternest test of love: forgiveness. A person who performs an act that calls for forgiveness is, in the first place, deserving of sympathy because of his state. Next, having done less than the noble thing, he must feel mortally hurt, and again this means that he is a candidate for forgiveness. Beyond that point, the one judging him is at fault and must learn to forgive himself. This complex necessity would never have appeared if there had already been enough love to cancel out the wrongdoing before it was committed.

When you forgive yourself for both judgment and blame, you pave the way for responsive forgiveness from others, and you correspondingly touch upon what Jesus must have felt at the peak of His test. That may have been His happiest moment on earth, for being a channel of love to such an extent must have been His greatest reward.

Putting It All Together

There is a notable change in today's world. I believe it results from our general awakening to the fact that there is no solidity — no dead permanency — in anything we see and touch. Rather, we marvel at the dynamic patterns that are functioning everywhere we turn. We are transformed into a race of the future because we have become aware of a never-ending series of opportunities that were not available in earlier years.

We used to acknowledge that a genius appeared in history every few centuries (how often have we quaked before the wisdom of an Aristotle!). Nowadays we encounter admirable intelligence on every doorstep. We are all showing unusual talents by means of the modern technology which signals subtle possibilities in the non-material realm. No longer confined within the five familiar senses, today we extend our faculties into previously unguessed dimensions. "The future need not happen to us; we can make it happen." And we emerge from the straitjacket of convention to undertake new tasks.

If we think of life as a river upon which we float toward the gleaming ocean, we find that Arthur, for instance, may become snagged against the submerged root of a tree along the shore, saying, "This is good enough for me." Why should he bother to extricate himself for the sake of continuing the journey downstream, when it is easy to stifle his curiosity as to what lies beyond the bend? Barry, on the other hand, enjoys the leisurely ride and says, "Things are going very well," not trying to hurry except within the sway of the current. But Colin with steady strokes covers as much mileage as he can, cooperating with the flow and manipulating cascades at intervals. Each has made his choice.

We can loiter while evolution takes centuries to introduce an improved species, or we can rapidly overtake the next juncture of circumstances.

While writing the life of Thomas Jefferson, Professor Dudley Malone of Columbia University observed that the third president of the United States not only was able to juggle politics while running the country but also had expert knowledge in several other fields of endeavor. What was the basis on which Jefferson surpassed so many others? Malone decided that the answer lay in the word *vigor*. Jefferson's vigor kept him constantly collecting information, increasing his drive, enlarging his horizon.

So Jefferson was one who swam ahead upon the river of life, extracting from the universe more and more energy, applying it more and more ardently, and repeatedly renewing his incentive.

On another level, surroundings are likely to initiate the right reaction. A young couple, falling in love, marry without realizing that they don't know how to raise a family; but when their children are born, they meet the occasion. What they need to know, they are taught by each rising situation. Had they halted out of fear of responsibility, they could never have become able to meet it. Those who remain in ignorance are not so much those who fail to know as those who fail to advance.

There was a boy named Howard Rusk, whose family had not the means to insure his education. Nevertheless, wanting to become a doctor from the age of eleven, he spent most of his childhood and youth finding ways to take part in the activities of a small-town hospital. He learned that if he cleaned the operating room he would be allowed to stay there while the surgeon was in action, and he daily absorbed knowledge of the profession he had chosen. By the time he had earned his license, his love for humanity had deepened to the point where it became his obsession to arrange for a special kind of care for cripples. He reasoned that a man whose legs were paralyzed nevertheless had other muscles that could be disciplined for activity. To effect this would require the spending of large sums of money for specially designed hospitals and technical equipment and for the training of enterprising doctors and nurses.

He could have said to himself, "I can't do anything about it because I haven't any money," and in that event he would have remained snagged by the submerged root of the tree along the shore.

But Dr. Rusk determined how much money would be needed for the appropriate architecture and services to operate a unique hospital. Then he made hundreds of speeches to selected audiences throughout the country. This effort gradually cultivated the inexplainable magnetism that drew to him the necessary resources. People who had accumulated fortunes in commercial enterprises went out of their way to help him realize his private vision. Because of his daring attitude, thousands of multiplegics in several countries have been trained for the satisfaction of self-help. The money used for that good purpose could have been spent otherwise, or some other doctor (if any other had thought of it) might have become the focal personality. It was Dr. Rusk who had the hardihood to swim ahead.

Bill Harder also wanted to become a doctor, but at college his grades in literature classes were better than his grades in chemistry. Therefore he was advised to become an English teacher, warned that he could never qualify for admission at any medical school. Naturally he was discouraged, as he confessed to Mr. Boyd, an older friend.

Mr. Boyd replied: "You are the only one who knows what is right for you. If you want to be a doctor, overcome obstacles as they arise and go on to your goal."

Bill said, "You are the only one who has spoken this way to me."

In fact, this one glimmer of advice that Bill wanted outweighed a ton of advice that did not suit him. He must have contrived in some way to satisfy his aim, for years later Mr. Boyd overheard this remark in a public place:

"My wife didn't get relief from any of the doctors we consulted, but one day I heard of a Dr. Bill Harder and we went to him. He gave my wife the first comfort she'd had since the accident."

You have a hunch about what you ought to do, and you can attract to yourself the support needed for its accomplishment. In the glorious scheme by which the suns and planets are swung, you are a part—a small part, admittedly. But every little notch must be in its own place; every little cog must fit into the right notch. How else could God's creation show its celebrated precision?

Never again need you believe that you exist in three dimensions (height, width, length) as a block of wood does. You are not a block of wood. You perform in more than three dimensions. Because your thinking is your own internal-combustion engine, you must keep it chugging by investing it with forward-leaning plans. Even the worm, "striving to be man, mounts through all spires of form," and the earth too, in its own striving, crumbles and erupts to a purpose. Every gesture is a catapult toward growth.

Your silent instruction, your own ESP, is the secret argument against friends who think they know better. Nobody else can realize why it is imperative that you obey your spirit (that department of you which for centuries was seldom known to exist). Your tentacles are delicately in touch with the eternity domain—the reservoir that Gustaf Strömberg, the astronomer, describes as holding forever the essence of all that is: past, present, and future.

Memory is a token of the past, telepathy is a token of the present, and expectation is a token of the future. Much of memory is stored away and seemingly forgotten, but any specific bit of it flashes out of the eternity domain when it is called upon by the human capacity. ("How did you know that?" your friends exclaim.)

As for the present, you may send your thoughts to a friend when he is miles away. If he is attuned to your frequency he later reports to you on the idea that you and he were sharing at that time.

"There is a power above and behind us," said Emerson, "and we are the channel of its communication."

Your thought is as steady as love and light and gravitation, the three elements that are never diverted except by deliberately placed obstructions. Your thought instantaneously reaches its target (even from off the earth, as was proved by Edgar Mitchell, the astronaut, during his trip to the moon).

Scientists systematically study natural forces, and almanacs record the start of seasons, the hour of sunrise and moonrise, the changes of tide. By using these inferences of the past, farmers are able to calculate a future: when and where to plant what, when and how to harvest. When and where to gather food from the ocean is learned from the past location of surface and subsurface creatures.

A fleet of technically equipped vessels annually collects millions of temperature readings from buoys set out on the ocean floor. By these the direction and the velocity of winds at various levels are traced for long-range weather forecasting and possible climate regulation. It is expected that eventually this information will enable us to tame hurricanes and control earthquakes.

Long ago, when there were scarcely a dozen trained oceanographers in America, one of them was driving me along the Pacific Coast, glancing occasionally at the plateau of white caps, and he said in a tone of deep feeling, "There is a reason for every motion of the ocean." I admired his selfless sense of wonder, in contrast to my pity for another man who, during a transatlantic voyage, had been shaken like a reed in a current as he tremulously asked, "Doesn't the motion of the ocean affect your morals?"

All these projects, even a study of the way our planet has evolved — geological history of the last hundred thousand years — result from our desire to construct the future. The stream of life upon which we float affords a constantly changing outlook. While we as the vast public accept our enlarged role, control by the elite diminishes. As a majority we take hold of our own destiny.

At the eighth annual festival of The International Cooperation Council, the vice-president of The Center for the Study of Democratic Institutions, Frank K. Kelly, spoke on the approaching success of the people in general to ban wars and other disunities, despite the sediment of the custom that a tribal chief or a feudal lord or an industrial official should arrange affairs for his own benefit:

Justification for the Universal Declaration of Human Rights rests upon increasing awareness of the immeasurable significance of each human person. . . . Nothing can halt the march of mankind toward reconciliation.

And he quoted the Russian author, Alexander Solzhenitsyn, who wrote, "The humble powers of all people are sustained by the everlasting flow of love."

So we welcome the trend by which history has been transcended through the developing adulthood of humanity. We no longer blindly follow the dictates of a self-appointed leader.

A recent article by H. James Birx, PhD, calls attention to the emphasis given by two outstanding scholars (Alfred North Whitehead and Albert Einstein) to the fact that all events are related "within the unity of the universe." That phrase is of course tautologous, but we have for so long made common use of the word *universe* that we have more or less forgotten its meaning (as we have forgotten the meaning of "Good-bye" and feel it necessary to affix the repetitive "Have a nice day").

Yes, historic-cultural conditions have long influenced us in our view of the universe with all its diversities, and they still substantiate the naturalistic and the idealistic aspects. It is only proper that we should assume a long perspective when we inhabit a globe that has been whirling around the sun for half a hundred million years, and the future must now be born out of all the past.

What we call technology has supplied us with equipment to withstand zero gravity in space as well as equipment to endure pressures at the bottom of the sea. In ordinary instances and also in contingencies considered miraculous, we find that inquiry is of use to us. Both experience in its simplest form and experience on the larger scene are justified by principles that have been seeping through the human mind ever since consciousness was injected into livingness. Many of these principles, mostly undefined, have been transmitted from generation to generation by means of automatic reaction.

Carl Jung suggested that matter is "only the objectivable manifestation" of something else, and this, he said, is not accessible to our investigation because we have no way of evidencing the combination of the psychic and the tangible. Often a mental impression and a physical event appear to be connected when they are not actually so. Their show of causal relationship may be merely an accidental reflection of a racial pattern plus action, independently inherited from long-lost origins. Thus, before we accept premonition as a cause or as a result of an occasion, we ought to consider that it may be no more than the casual intrusion of a detail from some unconnected branch of knowledge. That doubt delays us just when we believe we are deciphering the code.

One of Jung's discoveries, which he called "perhaps the most important key," was that imaginings are quasi-corporeal and quasi-spiritual "blended in an indissoluble unity." Surely there are frequent proofs that our environment and our achievements can be molded by our thinking. We shape our desire mentally, and in consequence we attain its reality. More and more we see that the psyche exerts influence upon the body, and vice versa. This synchrony between the ideal and its functional outcome leads us to trust the soul (or the prephysical if you prefer to call it that) to bring about "many things of the utmost profundity" outside the body as well as inside.

In the era when scientists were dedicated to the analysis of matter, no doubt it was because they assumed that matter was the only object that had to be examined. Now there is universal fascination with the psyche and its influence upon matter. Centering in the personal, a popular elaboration of immemorial prayer has recently been turning young people toward the Oriental habit of soliciting transcendent wisdom by silence, to foster peace and incidentally to heal bodily ailments.

Herbert Beierle, in a different but similar discipline, explains his healing technique in this way: "In treatment I visualize the patient's wholeness and thus effect wholeness within his consciousness."

He reported on his attendance at the First International Congress of Parapsychology and Psychotronics in Prague, during the summer of 1973. The assembly was composed of internationally known scholars representing fifteen scientific disciplines and, although Beierle had not been officially invited, one of the speakers asked him to go along. He was glad to do so, and he prepared a paper on mental healing in an offhand hope that he might be able to deliver it at one of the sessions. According to the rules, he placed that paper in the hands of the local censors and, because the communists promote only atheism, the paper was suspected of its opposite and was rejected.

Beierle said: "Divine order is always operating. If that paper ought to be read, it will be read at the right time."

Rumors of the rejection spread around the conference hall, and an Associated Press representative accepted these as news. Various members surrounded Beierle, calling him a healer—to his embarrassment, inasmuch as he insists that healing is done through him, never by him.

One man came forward and said, "Please heal the terrible bursitis in my right shoulder."

Beierle, more than willing to oblige, proceeded according to his usual five steps. First, he asked, "Do you believe in the power of the universe?"

"Yes, of course."

"Do you believe that this power works in you?"

"Yes, of course."

"Do you believe that the universe was

created perfect and that this perfection applies to you?"

"Ye-es," more hesitantly.

"You were created as a perfect idea, and you are healed right now."

"Really?"

Then Beierle arrived at the fifth step. "We are thankful for this healing. All sense of bursitis is now released from you. Lift your right arm."

"But it hurts to lift it."

"Lift it!"

The man lifted his right arm, and was so pleased at the cure that he swung it about and exclaimed and went around telling people.

Eight or ten others came to Beierle pleading for a treatment, and he said to each: "You are now healed of whatever it was that you no longer want to experience. Be thankful for this healing that has come through your own consciousness."

Most unexpectedly, one of the officials came to Beierle and said, "Give your paper now, please."

Of course Beierle complied, not inquiring the reason for the change in authority, not even learning whether he was being used to fill some vacancy in the program. He merely remembered that divine order, as always, was operating.

He said later: "Everybody in that part of the world thinks that Americans live in great prosperity. They asked me, 'How does it feel to own two cars and to get all the food you want to eat?' I answered: 'Just keep that consciousness. We accept your claim for us.' That whole nation is thinking positively about us, doing our creative work for us."

Each of us is a melding of the mental and the physical, and frequently one group or another inaugurates a communal attempt to execute improvement in public affairs. In this way thousands of people, silently and singly, in compliance with their separate dedications, can reach the hidden vein of the collective unconscious and assert their will for good. Such a modest movement is only a hint of the power now being wielded to reconcile all peoples and establish the overall well-being from which everyone will profit equally.

No doubt you too have been drawing satisfaction from the universal change.

Redeeming Memory

The most satisfying definition of the Creator that I have ever encountered is in a book by Buckminster Fuller. In a long paragraph composed of words that would send any reader to the dictionary, he speaks of "the Universal Intellectual Integrity spoken of as God, the most economical term thus far intuitively formulated by humanity to identify such an inspiring relationship."

As a matter of fact, he has not left out anything. But I find myself clinging to the word *integrity* because that is my favorite of the characteristics of the universe. How could there be a more reasonable explanation for the precision that drives the suns and planets? Even when applied to the activities of the errant human race within the Allness, integrity fundamentally describes what we must endure and that upon which we depend. It is the underlying truth that responds to our actions and comforts us by its authority.

Whatever seems whimsical in nature can no longer be so labeled when once it has been subjected to investigation. Scientists will never be without reason to study because the inquiring mind will never overtake all phases of reality, and every proven premise presents us again and again with further evidence of soundness.

One of the recent discoveries in psychology is that a sensible balance can correct the torture of regret by eliminating the anonymous cause of self-doubt. A recognition that the abuse of childhood is responsible for adult worries has engendered a movement to reprogram memory in order to release the present for the sake of constructing a wise future.

August Strindberg said, "If old age could

be free of the injustice done in childhood, it would be sweeter, but the pain and sorrow remain." Without having given his remark much credence, in order to cure contemporary difficulties we are now bringing into discussion the striving of a child within the womb and its horror at being catapulted into life's challenges. It is said that depression in adults is often the remainder of these unconsciously remembered trials. One of my friends tells me that she sometimes reminisces (when about to fall asleep) on the joys of rocking in the shelter of her mother before the sad parturition.

Today seminars are being held (in and out of churches) for the psychological healing of stresses that have lingered when supposedly forgotten. The meaningless affront or the inexcusable pretense that cripples a personality can now be analyzed, and the basis for discord is being changed to match the overall integrity.

Once upon a time there was a young oak tree who in one mood was ashamed of its acorn infancy and in another mood was intimidated by the big trees around it. Sometimes it stretched its young boughs in an effort to make believe it too was an old oak, but at other times it belittled the taller trees, pretending to be superior to them in quality if not in quantity. Of course it would never have acted in this reprehensible manner if only it had been as clever as people. . . .

Oh, yes, there actually are people who decry their past and are dissatisfied with their present and try to hasten their future. Perhaps the most devastating mental habit is self-commiseration over what formerly was done or was not done, if no excuse for self-pity can be invented.

Time was when I too was weighted with sorrow about past deficiencies . . . until I came to realize that self-chastisement is a human failing, not reserved for me alone but widely distributed. Thereupon I came to see that at any given time I had done the best possible with the equipment at hand, that remorse had set in only after I was operating under entirely different conditions and observing from a more experienced viewpoint.

The Nobel Prize novelist, Albert Camus, portrayed one of his anti-heroes as concluding that his life had been lived properly, for he had done what he was impelled to do according to his natural inclination, despite pressures that surrounded him. Complete detachment from convention made it natural for him to look with contentment upon his drab career, even when facing execution. There has been a great deal of comment on this philosophy of self-dependence, but most of us have not reached such a milestone of indifference. We must learn to erase unpleasant memories in our own way.

I was acquainted with Harry Winters when he first became certain that prayer could cause a desired event to happen in the future. Subsequently he stumbled upon the idea that if there were no such thing as time, the same process could work in reverse. In the first place, nothing is impossible to the Power that created us. Second, everything takes place simultaneously, inasmuch as there is no time except in our personal concepts. Thus what we call the past is amenable to change as well as is the future.

By employing this principle against his regret, Harry Winters could see no distinction between past and present or between present and future. So the particular moment when he had performed an injustice against a Mr. Conninger ought to be corrected right now. He dared to claim that the incident which rankled could be reduced to its native nothingness.

Does that seem a bit of mental acrobatics? He was willing to try it. And he actually made a move to eradicate the memory of his rudeness to Mr. Conninger, praying (in his unorthodox fashion) that it should simply no longer be in his experience in any way, shape, or form.

Within a week or two, "by coincidence" Harry Winters was at a party where the hostess innocently introduced him to Mr. Conninger as though they had not already met. Mr. Conninger had no recollection of having seen him before. Any wrong that may have been perpetrated was thus obliterated, and a completely new relationship bloomed between the two men.

There are as many angles from which to consider the past as there are human beings. One approach that might have become dangerous was exhibited by Leo Nash. He took pleasure in reciting anecdotes that showed him in the role of a lover with a flair for disappointing women. For a while this seemed his harmless way of picturing himself as popular, but one day I realized that he was reporting true instances of his willful cruelty against the opposite sex.

I said, "Leo, why don't you take a course of treatments at some psychiatric clinic?"

In a rage he demanded, "Why do you say such a thing to me?"

"Because you seem to be trying to punish your mother whenever you meet a girl," I answered. "I don't see why you should be troubled about your mother to that extent. You were kind to her when she was living, so your conscience ought to be clear. Maybe a psychiatrist could uncover your trouble."

"Why don't you treat me yourself?"

"Because I'm not charging a professional fee, and therefore you wouldn't be likely to take any benefit."

Leo did not want to spend money on a psychiatrist, but he did want to get rid of whatever in his past had built his hostility toward women. Finally he engaged in a bit of retrospection and confided in me.

His father, he explained, had always done whatever his wife told him to do. She would tell him to get their daughter's car from where the daughter had parked it upon leaving town, and he would oblige. She would tell him to buy certain commodities for the household when he was downtown, and he would not forget to do so on his way home from work. Each time Leo heard such an exchange between his parents he wanted to roar in anger, and he despised his father for doing what he was told to do, while despising his mother for being so officious.

"My mother ought to have been serving father instead of the other way around," he claimed in sincere chauvinism.

Quietly I asked, "Did your mother keep

house for your father, and cook for him, and nurse him when he was sick, and did she show love for him in other ways?"

"Of course," said Leo, "but that was only right."

My subsequent silence seemed to jar Leo, and his attempt to ransom his blame of his father by hostility to girls had at last collided with its answer. I hope it led him to improve his behavior.

As an example of a different nature, for many years Sheila went around mourning the death of her mother. She said: "I was only eighteen and didn't know what to do. If only I'd not been so ignorant, I might have found a way to save my mother's life."

Upon interrogation Sheila admitted that she had personally called upon a famous specialist to whom she was a stranger. She had enlisted his promise to treat her mother—"if you can move her to the hospital where I can see her every day," the doctor had stipulated.

Sheila borrowed money for an ambulance, rode in it with her mother to the specialist's jurisdiction, then earned money to meet the hospital expenses. Her mother died, nevertheless, and a relative paid the specialist's fee.

Well, then, why have regrets? If the famous specialist was unable to save her mother, it must have been because her mother was ready to go on to the next cycle. Why should Sheila continue to castigate herself for her quite understandable inability to do more?

"But I should have worked a miracle, because I loved her so!" Sheila protested.

While she was saying this a change came over her face, and it was clear that she was recognizing her egotism. Should she have changed every rule in the world to satisfy herself? There was certainly a reassessment in her revised view of the situation that had been harassing her.

When a young Lebanese woman was speaking about her father's homeland that had been ravished by invaders, suddenly she cried, "And I'm going back there some day to buy back my father's home."

Because she seemed to be uncannily involved, and because her husband was seriously pursuing a career in this country, I was afraid that she might some day disrupt her marriage in her infatuation with the past.

I said: "My mother's ancestral home in the South was plundered by the Union army during the Civil War. If I should now try to buy back that property at its present worth, it would mean not only the spending of many thousands of dollars but also the destruction of modern enterprises. You can see that sometimes it is better to let the past flow on."

My friend thought this over for a moment and then replied: "Oh, I was just talking. I guess I never did mean to do it." But the memory had needed to be expelled.

When we salvage all the energy wasted on self-incrimination we unveil the truth instead of prolonging the phantom of hurt feelings. We often find the adjective *universal* associated with the noun *truth* (as though truth could ever be anything but unlimited!), but perhaps a more exact adjective would be *hardy.* There is something irresistibly strong about the truth. It meanders through twisted channels to bob into sight at unexpected moments. There is no stopping its persistent pressure, especially where stubbornness has been mistaken for principle.

Like an ever-renewing tide, truth respects no blockage, despairs of no disappointments, merely proceeds without regard for centuries or distances. That is why it can be a solution to the conundrum of the past when we quit indulging our subconscious desire for justification, for martyrdom.

Let us confess that in the past our crowns were rather lopsided, our wits not equal to the occasion as we now wish they might have been. Moreover, let us acknowledge that today's ideal is different from the task of the past. Instead of decorating the past with a vain pose, we can bless it for having been an apt teacher. When we discard the contorted recollection and stop belaboring it with excuses (and a will to hurt someone in private revenge), we can see that the past was good within its own function.

Only a perspective beyond human possibility can give us this blessed remedy, and for this reason we resort to the "Universal Intellectual Integrity spoken of as God."

Intuition to the Rescue

Scholars are making progress in their search within the cosmic design for a clue to nature's effect upon our daily living. A recent discovery leads to the report that each creature develops according to its own eternal life-field that is present at the moment of birth.

As Dr. Harold Burr of the Yale University School of Medicine explains: "These fields are the basic blueprints of all life. We are beginning to see that the universe is a profoundly meaningful and orderly system, and so are we."

It has long been acknowledged that the human brain, by means of electrochemical reaction, involves the response of nerves and muscles. This knowledge can be applied for personal and collective benefit, when it is realized that the nervous system can be influenced by outer conditions and that the pulsing brain in its turn originates both alertness and fatigue. The self has got to determine which it shall be.

Well, what we call the laws of nature have been so named because of what we have observed. We are no longer confused as the primitives were by thunderstorms and forest fires, for we have found nature to be consistent and we count on it to act dependably. We have also found by experience that prayer is the one thing to circumvent the natural processes with which we are acquainted. No doubt prayer itself is typical of natural forces, but we are not yet able to trace it on its journey from here to there. No matter what it represents, a "soul's sincere desire" does attract a result, and our object is to use it for self-improvement.

The medical profession can now restrain diseases that once ravaged the population. Vaccines and other preventive measures protect the public health, and many a deformity can be corrected by new surgical procedures. Besides, scores of other difficulties that used to be considered unavoidable calamities are now bridled by scientific methods. But it still happens that frequently we are confronted by a situation that puzzles the best of us.

On such an occasion, often in desperation we resort to prayer. Regardless of the words we use or the bargain we may try to strike by promising to be good, the value of the prayer appears in the way it carves a swath through space and time, breaking through the human barrier to reach the reservoir of creation. Innately we entertain a standard of rightness that we believe everyone ought to enjoy, and by means of prayer we invite the ideal to assert itself in tangible circumstance.

Even a doctor (perhaps I should say, especially a doctor who knows the obstacles to cure) recognizes what is temporarily called a miracle when a patient develops a "new lease on life." But to the cosmic performance there can be no mystery in restoration of normality. Perhaps the appearance of a wrong is always due to human myopia. Yet until now it has been hard for us to realize that the advantage of prayer coincides with the so-called laws of nature.

Many of our casually accepted pursuits are every bit as surprising when we stop to consider them. For instance, everybody admits that we think, and what could be more stupendous than that? The mind is something different from the brain: it is the mind that instructs the gray matter in order to cause it to think.

We can decide upon an action and secure the precise movement of the proper muscles to execute that action. With amazing dexterity our hands can execute tasks, our vocal cords can manipulate speech, and even the heartbeat and blood pressure can be hurried or slowed by concentration upon such visceral motion. The energy we induce within us impels us to obey thought, and thought is upon a track far different from function.

In trying to determine what motivates thought, we hope to pounce upon the secret of healing that follows prayer. Matter alone could not make such a change, for flesh has no initiative. Although tests are made to determine the obedience of body cells, whose commands do they obey?

There are countless examples of the way a person's mental propensity sways his physical state, and we no longer doubt the relationship between the two. Not long ago, during a lecture, Dr. Carl Simonton produced a series of photographs showing a cancerous growth in various stages of healing. The disease was gradually eliminated while the patient worked at persuading himself that his body's "good" cells could outnumber the marauding cells in battle. When the final picture of the series was thrown on the auditorium screen, it showed such healthy tissue that all the viewers vibrated in celebration, although the patient was a stranger and nameless. We were all taking it personally!

In my neighborhood there was a less tragic but equally symbolic instance: An old woman became sick enough to spend a day or two lying on a couch. I said to her ten-year-old grandson, "Is your grandmother feeling better today?" He replied in satisfaction,

"No, but my grandfather will be home on Sunday." The child understood that an improvement in his grandmother's health would take place at sight of her husband, who had been absent for several weeks. Of course he was right, as her Sunday disposition testified.

Long after we have accepted the fact that a patient's emotion affects his body, we continue to ask, "How can this be true?"

Moreover, how can some thoughts not within the patient's own mind govern him, as in healing treatment across distance? Is this done by something like radio frequency? Even in a social gathering, one guest may make us feel cheerful while another may depress us. The personality of another does touch upon our feelings and often upon our health. Undoubtedly thoughts are things, and minds are linked by some means, even though we are not yet able to explain the process reliably.

"Well, then, it must be an invisible connection."

"How do we know it is there if we can't see it?"

"Oh, let the results speak for themselves."
So goes the dialogue.

Fervent prayer is our strongest mode of thinking. It is a proclivity by which, in some still unproven manner, we direct thought undeviatingly toward some replenishing fountain. As far as we know, it is necessary for the ego to surrender in order to be separate from time and space and thus become free from material obstruction. By stepping aside from our three-dimensional self — by releasing self-interest — we allow the fourth dimension to take over. Then, electrically or otherwise, we contact the central source in which rightness resides.

We must merely learn to avoid the blockage by becoming enthusiastically willing that the correction shall be made (and willing is an active operation, not mere amiability). Actually, this amounts to a recognition of ESP, and most of us are beginning to make practical use of that, for there is no longer ridicule to deter us from admitting our hunches.

The English writer, Rosalind Heywood,

tells of the time during her pregnancy when she was extremely tired with no apparent reason. While she gave herself the privacy to think about it, she had a sudden vision of the chalky white cliffs of Dover, along with a wordless hint that her diet lacked calcium. She followed the implied suggestion to reprogram her meals, and soon regained her vigor.

When I read this, I recalled how one morning I found myself unusually weary and doubted that I could complete the day's agenda. In asking a silent question, immediately I became aware of a word that I had at that time never before heard: *riboflavin*. I looked it up in the dictionary, where it was explained as a growth-promoting member of the vitamin B complex. That reminded me that I had been neglecting meals for several days. After I indulged in a hearty breakfast, my strength was adequate for the day's work.

At that same "point in time" there was another incident in line with health through ESP. After my little wire-haired terrier had run through the poison-oak bushes, I lifted her to carry her over a tidal wave and, as a result, my forearms became infected from her coat. While I was wondering what to do, inside my head, as though a voice were speaking there, I heard the words, "carbolic acid." That chemical had not been mentioned in my hearing since my childhood, and now I wondered how it could be acquired. Right away the inside sound changed to the name of a popular soap.

"Oh, yes, that soap does smell like carbolic acid," I said aloud.

So I rubbed some of its suds upon my forearms and had quick relief. (Unfortunately the formula for that soap has been changed.)

There have been numerous examples of intuitive information that led to cures, and the memories of such reports have accumulated as "folk medicine." One man tells me that his nurse kept his childhood free of injuries by her loving pat and calm declaration, "It's all right now." The rubbing of gold against an eye as a cure for a sty has often been called "nothing but superstition," and yet one woman's old-fashioned gold wedding ring cured many a sty on the eyes of her children and the children of her neighbors. The special worth of honey and lemon as tonic has been justified by good dietitians, and there are other "common sense" remedies that are no longer scorned.

Once I read a magazine article about a cancer patient who received an extrasensory impression that she ought to eat beets. She ate beets, beets, beets for several weeks, her constitution welcoming that food, to the amazement of her relatives. Finally her malignant tumor disappeared. The writer of the article cautioned readers not to expect such a prescription to have the same result for another. That is the beautiful thing about intuition: it pertains to one person at one moment, and (as the theologian Martin Buber warned in a wider context) every "revelation" is for its own particular moment, its own peculiar situation.

A hunch to stay at home has often saved a person from being caught in a fatal accident. In the same way, many a person has had a silent warning not to eat a food that later turned out to be harmful for his constitution.

This instinctive assistance for the inner need is like a whispering through the body, and it is wiser than we usually admit.

My friend Lee had been out of a job long enough to have lost some of his self-respect, and he conceived the idea of contacting a certain rich man to ask his assistance in inaugurating a new career. At his first bold approach to the stranger's office, he was secretly relieved to be told that the man he asked to interview was out of town. But the connection even that close to a symbol of success brought about an inner response that had evaded him earlier, "If I should tell him my qualifications he would reply, 'With such values you don't need me.' " This was a realization that may always have been available to Lee, but evidently its appearance in his consciousness had needed prompting. At last he was able to go forth and rely upon himself to create an opportunity for the use of his past experience.

The current wave of publicity that ESP has been receiving has encouraged suppressed individuals to speak out. Apparently the majority of people have been keeping quiet about that something within themselves which tries to protect them from mistakes — sometimes by a warning that a new acquaintance has less than a good influence, sometimes by the body's call for extra sleep to prevent an illness, sometimes by an inclination to change course and avoid danger. In a recent assembly, nearly a thousand men and women were questioned from the platform, "How many here have had helpful instances of ESP?" More than seventy-five percent of those present raised their hands.

As a people we are developing enough self-confidence to reap advantage from our most ancient faculty, now that it is at last being invited to enter the forefront of the brain. So the religious contingent will be justified in declaring, "That's what we've been telling you all along." When the advice to pray is flavored with denominationalism it arouses resistance, but when it is recognized as a reinforcement of the inner conviction we take heart.

One proof of the new recognition is the

contrivance known as the neural efficiency analyzer invented by Dr. John Ertl, director of the Center of Cybernetic Studies at the University of Ottawa. By a culture-free and motivation-free technique, it measures a subject's native ability to learn. Tests administered by means of this new method have uncovered a fundamental potential that has not previously been ascertainable. Hereafter, the quality of life can be enhanced as we turn sharper focus upon the innate understanding that imbues each character with the power to express its unique worth within any given environment.

If there had been knowledge of this centuries ago, the great poet Francis Thompson would have been honored for his "indolence" instead of flouted into poverty, and William Blake's genius would have been welcomed instead of discredited.

It is only as late as the closing third of the twentieth century that scientists have found the undercurrent reason for the variety in human nature. They now describe the lifefield that comprises the source of direction by which each living creature develops.

"The human body," says Joseph Goodavage, "is far, far greater than the sum of its components. Only the L-field can know the organism's needs in advance. Only the L-field can send the necessary substances to the right part of the body at the right time and maintain the constant pattern of the body for many years. The human body is not some miraculous exception to the universal law of energy fields."

Then is this underlying matrix the fountain into which prayer delves when we ask urgently for the basic best of ourself? Is this the center upon which we can rely for the mystic answer that is already ours before we ask? No wonder we have always been secretly convinced that the "soul's sincere desire" can rescue us in any emergency.

And, as always, nature is logical. "God provides" does not mean that He fails to grow the fruit and other foods by which we shall be nourished. "God answers" does not mean that He breaks the laws of the universe to construct a miracle. His care for us is imbedded within the life-field which He devised far ahead of time and to which we have immediate access. In our moments of meditation we draw upon the ready abundance that is contained in the special and personal life-field by which each of us is guided and sustained.

I do believe this is the secret: Our talent to pause and listen enables us to contact the provision already arranged for us before birth and everlastingly. No wonder, then, that we are able through prayer to take each promotion as we ask for it! No wonder, then, that only when we are ready for the next step do we ask for it!

The Long Reach of Telepathy

We can no longer deny the marvel of telepathy, because we have all met with at least a sample of it, even though we cannot explain it. We are surprised at its elastic possibilities, for we find it happening sometimes between close friends and sometimes between people far apart. We ask: "Do we receive the message that is sent to us, or do we ourself set the message in action? Must we ask before receiving it, or is it ready for us to receive before we think of asking?"

Most of us conduct our affairs as well as we can, and we hardly ever try to stretch our imagination. However, when we face a problem that we don't know how to solve, we yearn toward a wider horizon and try to reach a higher wisdom. It is then that we experience a miracle of rescue. When that happens, in a tone of wonder we explode with a report to our friends: "My husband became well before morning!" or "The morning mail brought the exact amount of money I needed!" or "My friend found out that I hadn't betrayed his confidence after all!"

At such a moment, we are so well satisfied that we vow we shall never again "bother the angels"—until another sorrow outdistances our power and we feel forced to make another appeal. That is our own brand of telepathy, and whether or not it reaches over vast space we do not know. Maybe the answer is nearer than hands and feet.

Often we are tempted to try to define the process so as to be able to make use of it later. We ask: "How did we find a solution so quickly? Was it because we had to find it?" This is a normal question among the young as well as the old—and even among the in-betweens, too, especially if they are scientists looking for repeatable results.

Fervent discussions on how to overtake mysterious information are held at international conferences where scholars assemble to exert a collective inquiry. Their enthusiasm can almost be felt, like velvet. But unfortunately, frequently at such events the discipline of the laboratory has dulled the novelty of their ideas. In an effort to be logical they backstep by supposing, "The solution may not be attainable after all." That negative attitude doesn't help much, as you can imagine.

On one such occasion Sir Alister Hardy, from his lofty status as professor emeritus of Oxford University, attempted to renew hope. He reminded, "In man's long history there has been evidence of a belief in an extrasensory contact with a Power which appears to be greater than the individual himself."

All the skeptics from many countries must have been horrified at such a daring statement. It came at a time when they were admitting that they represented more technique than success. Their so-called "objective" studies were showing more distraction than conclusion, and it was important for them to find another path to travel. Was their concentration focused in the wrong direction? Why else had they not arrived at the right solution? Were they going around in a two-dimensional circle, and was it now indicated that they must invade the third (or fourth) dimension?

And then Sir Alister continued: "Telepathy is the transmission of whole patterns of thought—independent of words. That ought to be our point of departure. Let us now recognize this faculty of communication, not only on the human plane but actually as a means of approaching the realm upon which we draw when we engage in prayer."

Fancy dragging in mention of *prayer* to a congregation of hard-boiled scientists! If this had been said by an unknown, it would have been labeled heresy, but Sir Alister was in a position to inspire respect.

One professor who follows the philosophy of Carl G. Jung immediately took the cue. He urged, "Let us reflect upon the psychic impetus of the field," and he definitely encouraged his colleagues to invest their time upon more than they could see and touch.

"In making an effort to control what is by nature spontaneous activity," he said, "maybe we are creating insoluble problems for ourselves. It may be a mistake to ignore something that transcends what we know as matter. Let us examine parapsychological happenings more open-mindedly."

Another scientist made this contribution: "Do our diligent tests in the laboratory actually cause the alleged phenomena to disappear?"

Other materialists then lined up with the hint that telepathy ought to be valued beyond our modest expectations: "It may even have its seat in age-old prayer, inasmuch as it enables us to draw upon more than human assistance."

Surely the assembly was now riddled with a new outlook. Their statistical charts, with clever curves upon them, were good on a two-dimensional level, but they had never supplied inspiration.

By now these scientists were beguiled to "become as little children." They had been depending upon intellectualism instead of upon heartwarming. Charles Honorton once quoted a nineteenth-century writer as saying that a certain explanation of psychology seemed "so preposterously silly it could only have been proposed by very learned men who were themselves too confused to know what they were saying." That problem could be avoided if they would court simplicity. It may only be necessary to accept the revelation of this planet—"decked with cloud and wind, rushing rivers and foaming seas, and the gorgeous finery of flora and fauna." Doesn't it tell us more than can be extracted from, say, a two-mile-long machine that is now being erected in the hope of intercepting the theoretical quark? No wonder Sir Thomas Browne once declared, "It would be better to work according to the ordainer of order and the mystical mathematics of the city of heaven."

If we want a sharper knowledge than our halting investigations provide, we shall have to respect the individual's attempt to blend with what is better than his own highest self. This returns the aspiration of the parapsychologists to the individual, in whom it is fortified during the long extension of life from the amoeba to the human species. In turning away from the test tube we realize that the definition of religion is no longer "the cry of the oppressed." It has now become "one of man's most fundamental forms of existence, his sense of the holy that will never disappear."

Only ignorance of inevitable nature has heretofore caused our failure to benefit by it. It does seem that, before we can advance, we must be blocked sternly enough to discover that we are on a detour. Then only can we surrender. When the situation seems to exercise great ingenuity against us, it makes us start over again. By necessity we stop relying on our limited perspective so that we may travel blithely along the more open road.

Once I was unwillingly jockeyed into making my home in beautiful Carmel-by-the-Sea, and it became a precious interlude. Why had I at first resisted it? After seven and a half years in Carmel, writing and editing and teaching, I had no intention of interrupting this idyl. In fact, I staunchly declined certain suggestions that I make a change.

But suddenly my financial resources dwindled away, and my friend the landlady (without consulting me) resorted to the law in an attempt to break my lease. Because of previous experience I recognized all this as a signal of some sort, but I was not easily swung out of the pleasant rut.

The one thing that prompted me to pay attention was a realization that I was being stubborn. In order to dissolve the wall I had erected around myself, I contrived to take time to listen. Within a few minutes the warm atmosphere of meditation embraced me, and inside my skull I heard the words: Go to New York. Go to New York.

Having been born and reared in New York and having decided that for me it was more desirable to live in the West, I certainly did not want to return to the metropolis. In fact, it was the last thing I wanted to do. Although

I had purposely taken this hour to ask for guidance, I was so full of self-will that I replied to the silent command with an excuse, "Oh, I can't do that because I don't have the fare." For a person who had countless times secured money for worthy purposes by consciously drawing upon invisible bounty, this was the rankest kind of pretense, and I now wonder that I was dishonest enough to perpetrate it.

But the quiet instruction persisted, and no alibi could quell it. Therefore I accepted it and suddenly felt more than at peace; I felt stimulated. I packed my possessions and wrote the landlady, agreeing to let her have her house without a struggle. Although my liquid assets were nil, the telepathic initiative that had alerted me left me without the slightest doubt that funds would be supplied at the proper time.

After nine o'clock that evening, I received a long-distance telephone call regarding a rewrite job that had to be done at once and that would pay me well. On the date I had agreed to vacate the house, I flew to New

York more than willingly—quite expectantly, as a matter of fact. And there such a volume of unexpected editing and writing fell to my lot that I had no time to think of leaving New York. . . .

Until another seven and a half years had elapsed. Then all of a sudden I had a sense that this chapter too was finished—that there was something else, somewhere else, that had to be done. And that turned out to be so.

The reward was a return to my beloved West Coast where again, in ways that I could not have foreseen, my literary services were in demand. I had by this time become convinced that Someone had advance knowledge somewhere about what had to be done by me. I knew also that, in order to adjust to wherever I belonged at any particular time, I would have to make use of telepathy from outside my usual range.

I am a pronounced advocate of free will, and I rejoice that each of us can choose the way to spend life. But sometimes it is wise to overcome an automatic resistance to change. This can be done by listening to the still small voice whose advice reveals a prospect much to be preferred.

Two-way telepathy, across elements that we scarcely know, can do more than tell us who is telephoning before we pick up the receiver (as many of our friends claim); more than direct us to turn a corner in order to come face to face with a person we need to meet (as Mark Twain related). We can also receive intimate instruction about how to fulfill some impersonal necessity, how to accomplish some unguessed task. First, the prayer we think of making is in response to a silent call; second, when we listen after praying we complete the connection.

This leads us into the most satisfying kind of happiness, and that is why, as one who has learned to practice it, I recommend the method to you.

In this way I am relating prayer to the use of telepathy, for the long reach of the mind is the only means by which we can touch the higher realm. Only in dedication to the right (regardless of personal bias), only in surrender to the wisdom beyond our own, can we find our release from limitation, and our ultimate contentment.

The New Independence

Two hundred years ago, the chick of humanity pecked at the shell of royalty and stepped forth into the dangers of democracy. A daring document called the Declaration of Independence was formulated by a handful of men who had brains and courage. Their countrymen accepted it because they had by then evolved to the point where nothing less could have matched their capacities.

Since then we have made a further progression and are ready for a new consideration. It is therefore not surprising that many books as well as newspaper and magazine articles are proclaiming the recent breakthrough into psychic and other humanistic discoveries. Men and women who have never before thought of anything more than food and fuel are suddenly awakened to the fact that they have better possibilities.

To celebrate his eightieth year, Dr. J. B. Rhine, precursor in the scientific investigation of mental fields, undertook a nationwide speaking tour. As he addressed several overflowing symposia on the topic of newly confirmed human traits, he was able to scan more than half a century of academic opposition. Only as recently as 1969 was his studious method justified. During that year the august American Association for the Advancement of Science invited parapsychologists to apply for membership. That was the first scholarly acknowledgment of the invisible qualifications that Dr. Rhine and his wife had painstakingly striven to define. At long last his pioneering was vindicated—and it was as if a valve was abrupty released, for a wealth of vitality spurted forth, apprising the public of values long stifled.

In characteristically sweet-tempered optimism, Dr. Rhine made this dynamic suggestion: "Let us now issue a declaration of independence of the human mind against the tyranny of materialism."

We are now independent of the "practical" shackles that thwarted us in earlier centuries. We are self-reliantly entering an era for which we have been unconsciously preparing. We know that as a race we are a channel for the life essence of original creation, and we slough off the long-term denial of our divinity. As recipients of the godly inheritance, we can now extend our understanding beyond the boundary of the five senses within which we were heretofore expected to remain enclosed.

In looking backward (over not only the last two hundred years, but also over a million previous), we do discover that we "have come a long way," as a certain quaint ad reminds us. But a popular song croons, "We've only just begun," and the vistas ahead show us that this is true. The English poet Walter de la Mare said that what we are evolving from is of much less significance than what we are evolving into, and our automatic yearning for the future proves this. Even if merely because of curiosity about what may happen next, we tingle in anticipation. We gauge the value of every chance to advance, and we try not to let our obstinacy postpone a good prospect.

Just the same, often we do show a "passionate reluctance" to implement something new. Until we learn how constructive "mere" thoughts are, we reject anything that seems to be imaginary. Actually, we ought not to shy away from any inference of the unusual. Every fleeting idea appears first in the gray matter. Intuition itself is one of the brain's products, while *rapport* between two persons or between two locations is only part of the good old human aptitude to adjust.

Those who refuse to find worth in what cannot be seen or touched are likely to say that no person can learn a foreign language or run a four-minute mile, only because neither is done by everyone always. Every extension of competence seems impossible until it is demonstrated. But as we become used to our new functions, we are simply displaying an additional feature of evolution.

Not only the uneducated sneer at new contingencies. A short time ago some federal official appointed the late Dr. Edward U. Condon, a renowned theoretical physicist, to determine whether or not UFOs had been seen as rumored. Without a qualm (I am sure), he announced that there were no such things as UFOs. He was completely confident of his intellectuality, as anyone might have been after having been acclaimed by scholars ever since his youth. Without even attempting to explain the meaning of the term UFO, he relied upon his personal judgment, and that, unfortunately, did not promote the study. In a past life he may have been one who said the alchemists were foolish to expect to analyze the elements of metal; or in a later period he may have been one who insisted that only bleeding could cure ailments.

Dr. Barbara Brown of the University of California, Los Angeles, during her dinner speech at an annual convention, maintained, many have failed to measure so-called psychic reaction because sometimes the researcher negates a possible disclosure if it does not correspond with his conviction. She says, "I have invariably found physiologic and/or brain-wave changes during psychic activity; when I have turned the experiments over to other people, they have not found them."

A systematic procedure surely ought to comprise an account of the experimenter's bias as well as a statement of the problem to be solved. You know every new notion meets with suspicion; so why should we try to hurry the recognition of the mind's new range?

Psychologists have learned that there is an "innate perception pattern" in each individual at birth; that characteristic preferences arise in every personality. Despite the numerous individual differences, all that takes place lies within the action initiated by Creation itself: the universal principle establishes itself through every move we make. Each of us has personal equipment that performs in our daily affairs, helping us to focus correctly even when we delay. Eventually we move on to each plane of our destiny as we are ready for it.

Our never-to-be-discouraged pilgrimage is within the stream by which nature guides us to a culmination, even while we do not see it. This drive resides in matter (what else?), having been originally instilled in the available organs and nerve centers. Animal life thrusts toward the advent of man, and man struggles to manifest divinity.

Dr. Stanley Dean (of the University of Florida Medical School) has said, "There is importance in realities that are beyond perceptual or intellectual apprehension," and some of these realities are now accessible to the public because of the patient experiments by the Rhines and many others. They show us why we persevere in aspiration. Dr. Edgar Mitchell also speaks of "an unseen dimension behind the visible creation" that leads us everlastingly to transcend whatever we have been.

Our transformation is continuous, in line with our gradually transformed relationship with the cosmos. Within a universe that is nonspatial and nontemporal, we are always becoming more and more knowledgeable. Modern technology, as it unfolds, expresses our inner depth in the form of outward experience.

Insight appeared in our evolution before we could visualize our present ideal. Today it enables us to shape our environment which, in turn, invigorates our intentions and our will to act. With our current vision of a collective mankind, we harness collective energy toward a collective goal. Never before has there been such teamwork and sacrifice of personal prominence to the general good.

In realizing that we are all encircled together, we have amplified our total resonance into a future for which we have hungered. Singly we were unable to wield authority enough to maneuver the various levels of substance. Now jointly we intertwine all aspects in order to overtake higher potential. In combination, we are a force that reduces the individual's internal stress while strengthening the total purpose.

For too long we could see only each personal contribution, without being able to project the whole scene. Now we have the means by which we can harmonize. What we have been craving we are on the verge of attaining, because the physical sciences have found the design that religion has always claimed as existent.

At last science and religion embrace. All that has been admitted by one has become imbedded in the other, each in the language of its own unique psychology. Abstruse matters are converted into fact; fact is the mainstay of faith. Both groups have been traveling in the same direction, and now on the shore of a promising continent they unite. It is no longer necessary for us secretly to believe in magic, as formerly. We have overcome the barrier of materialism to the extent that we see it immersed in the "super" natural.

Who was it who first said, "'Tis love that makes the world go 'round"? Was that remark an attempt at wit, or did the speaker have an inkling of its profundity? And why did we ever take it for granted that love was a talent that had to be motivated by a human being? Often we have been advised to love as though it were in our power to spark the flame.

But all the time, what we innocently called love was *coordination,* the foundation stone of the cosmos. This is the basic relationship of all souls in all endeavors, as exemplified in the astronomical system and as permeating every living thing. It is never something for us to choose; rather, it is an imperative. But heretofore our outlook has been clouded by fear. We used to think that the little self had to be protected from all else. We used to think that the misdirection of greed had to be indulged. At present the desire for universal good encourages us to cordial exchange.

Assuredly, the march has been long and slow. We traversed a myriad of experiences before we suspected that we are all moving along the eternal way.

On this subject Charles Lindbergh once reminded us that wheels introduced land travel, hulls enabled us to cover the sea, and wings opened the sky for our exploration. Then he carried the analogy into man's exercise to "merge with the miraculous" (to which we can attach what better name than God?).

And he continued:

"Will we then find life only a stage, though an essential one, in a cosmic evolution of which our evolving awareness is beginning to become aware? I believe it is through sensing and thinking about such concepts that great adventures of the future will be found."

I am willing to take a cue from him and exclaim, "How glorious it is that we have only just begun!"

In obedience to Dr. Rhine's instruction, we declare our independence from materialism and rejoice in our delivery from the old hindrances of dogma and doubt. From here forward we remember who we are: the inheritors of the realm in which God's will is fulfilled, to our perpetual health and happiness. We put our shoulders to the wheel and press forward. Mankind has come from afar and is now able to do greater things.

Ever since my adolescence I have been reinforced by a quotation from Lord Dunsany, and I offer it here as a resolution for us all:

"These were as nothing compared with those things which in their youth they had dreamed and which they mightily purposed yet to do."

Let's go! The future is ours.

A Look at the Past

When the United States of America was one hundred years old, Walt Whitman challenged the citizenry by inserting in his annually expanding book, "Leaves of Grass," these questions:

Who are you indeed who would talk or sing to America?

Have you studied out the land, its idiom and men?

Have you learn'd the physiology, phrenology, politics, geography, pride, freedom, friendship of the land? its substratums and objects?

Have you consider'd the organic compact of the first day of the first year of Inde-

> *pendence, sign'd by the Commissioners, ratified by the States, and read by Washington at the head of the army?*
>
> *Have you possess'd yourself of the Federal Constitution?*
>
> *Do you see who have left all feudal processes and poems behind them, and assumed the poems and processes of Democracy?*
>
> *What is this you bring to my America?*
>
> *Does it answer universal needs?*

You can see the pride with which he spoke as an American, and how he thought that all Americans should become engaged in satisfying universal needs.

Now after our two hundredth year we can ask the same questions and face up to our responsibility. Belonging to this country gives us a platform from which to speak with resolution. We can assume the power that such belonging bestows upon us and become architects of the future, as none of us could ever do alone. Collectively we are obliged to take up the joyful task.

The other day a man of my acquaintance

said to me: "I thought I was all alone. I worked my way through college, and then I could have stayed on to get a doctor's degree in philosophy, but I wasn't willing to spend another three years drudging—'all for what?' I asked myself. But years later my grandfather said to me, 'I was disappointed that you didn't continue your studies,' and without thinking I blurted out, 'I'd have gone on if I'd known it mattered to you.' That was the first time I realized what strength there is in having a family. If I'd known anybody cared, I'd have exerted the extra effort."

While he was telling me this I pondered on the difference it makes in a person's life if he believes there is nothing to exact his loyalty. And what value there is for character building when patriotism bolsters a personal program! Anyone without a country is indeed a flat picture—no background to draw upon, no reason for dedication. Certainly the importance of this country's birth on grounds of fair representation in lawmaking stands out as an undeniable inspiration. It gives us something to live up to.

Whitman was right in urging us to study the land and the idiom; to learn the geography and appraise "the compact of the first day of the first year." How else can we rise to the worth of citizenship in this remarkable precedent of freedom—especially freedom to criticize the government, as most of us delight in doing!

Recently the ripe maturity of the United States has revealed the greater depth that her people are demanding of government practitioners. Never before has there been such unanimity among the populace (and never before has there been such a numerous populace, either). Hereafter, honor must be the gauge of public service. This is now specified by the majority of our people, and it is one of the finer instruments being honed for the advance of the whole human race.

Often before, in the length of history, there have been heights of attainment, but there have been frequent inundations also, when only the outstanding souls in each century longed for perfection. However, now there is widespread call for the betterment that previously was suspected as possible by only the few. There is no doubt that today's expectations have been nurtured by those with foresight enough to replace with constructive thinking the rigid dogmas of past generations. People are now accepting the enlarged promise, for the unlimited universe has been introduced to us and such a great enterprise awakens us to the fact that we are not "little people" boxed in. So we are taking the initiative in asking for what the higher consciousness has been prescribing.

The practical results of our affirmations are visible: there are new advantages to be had, and we now claim them. But it is true that we have only gradually arrived at this particular milestone.

There was, at first, consternation among many of us when unsupervised youth began to use drugs in their desire to widen their outlook. This underground movement was only a natural exaggeration of what they had observed in their elders. Alcohol and nicotine and caffeine appetites had long been the refuge of many who hoped to elude their daily troubles by as much of an opiate as they were willing to sample. When experiments with hallucinative drugs were undertaken, it was for the purpose of contacting the illusion of a great new prospect. The daring young ones made the experiment.

Unfortunately, like every adventure, it had its dangers. Travelers used to be lost at sea, but that did not stop exploration; better equipment and wiser handling were devised, and today there is abundant safety for travelers. And so it must be with those who want to court higher consciousness instead of continuing to be circumscribed by the advice of their failed ancestors.

No doubt it was this mistaken stab at a quick reply to aspiration which has led to present-day practices—for many of those very experimenters are nowadays devoted to the discipline of silent prayer alongside positive attitudes.

"What you are like," said Evelyn Underhill, "is going to depend upon your life of prayer."

These days, then, a new element is entering into our population.

She continued, "Perhaps all earth's lesser demands and vocations, the sacrificial call of truth and beauty, the passion of the explorer or the mountaineer, overriding selfishness and ease, are part of the intricate process by which souls are trained for the supreme self-giving of eternal life."

The rising generation is surely listening *within* for leadership, and it is already obvious that they are manifesting a healthy balance. They are investing the self wisely, learning to live affirmatively—and learning to like it.

"We know, by intuition, that there is something beyond what we have so far consciously experienced," Ernest Holmes once said.

The meditators no longer lean exclusively upon the intellect and no longer confine their activities to the reports of the five senses. They consider less of the outward form and more of the inner layer, and therefore they are guarded against materialism even while enjoying fruition of their endeavors. Besides, in celebrating similarities instead of differences among people, they are protected from the ego that brews despair. This correction in the method of operating (personally and politically but also internationally) will open the way to flashes of intuition and to recognition of the liberation that timelessness provides—not only for individuals but for nations and continents as well.

Of course this innovation has to begin with you and me. A sensory experience is often unmatched by logic, and it is often elevated into emotion as it draws attention to the lasting essence behind all that is experienced. Many memorable events are unexplainable. For instance, despite a scholarly accumulation of data, many a scientific discovery has been encountered not through such data but actually by their interpretation in a moment of guileless relaxation. In the same way improvement in human living is confronted.

Friedrich Nietzsche said: "One can hardly reject completely the idea that one is the mere incarnation, or mouthpiece, or medium of some almighty power. One hears—one does not seek; one takes — one does not ask who gives: a thought flashes out like lightning, inevitable without hesitation."

In this particular phase we are becoming worthier of the country that harbors us. Our naive public requirement of pledging allegiance to the flag is a reversion to the time after the Civil War when there was a political reason for that exercise, but it has imbued us with subconscious faith in the alliance of all citizens. (Once I was out of the country for ten days, and my sudden sight of the Stars and Stripes threw me into a rapture.)

In our resultant strength we can relax from the outmoded necessity of selecting what we want without realizing that its opposite must accompany it. We can thus avoid the dualism that originally caused many a struggle. When we accept the full equation instead of resisting nature, we experience a transcendence over conflict. No pattern can be as contradictory as fear of the unknown has made it seem, and what actually occurs is acceptable while we cooperate. And cooperate we must when we see the whole picture with each side of an argument in the right.

The secret of success lies in relying upon the facility to let go, to let happen, to allow understanding to take its course. World peace will eventually follow universal willingness to partake of a gracious infinity, and this is the aspect we glimpse during the exercise of listening to the Within.

The history of our country has not always exemplified the mystic, but the Declaration of Independence was composed by men who depended upon answer to prayer while they knew they might be executed as traitors; the Constitution was assembled under the guidance of prayer. Besides, the prosperity of this nation is nothing to be ignored, and you know how consistently our money is marked with signs of faith in God.

The only value of a look at the past is its suggestion that we may surpass it in our structure of the future. As individual citizens improve themselves, they confer greatness upon their country. That, at present, is our dearest project.

Today's Evolution

It is exciting to discover that we are continually moving from one rung to another, pressed higher and higher as life carries us onward. We especially enjoy taking our own initiative in this process.

One of my longtime friends, a member of the Women's Overseas Service League, spent her life serving not only her country but also persons young and old. Her name became known to so many that wherever I happened to be I might ask, "Do you know Rose Glass?" and the answer invariably was, "I should say I do!" This is the advice she gave:

Bite off more than you can chew and chew it.

Tackle more than you can do and do it.
Hitch your wagon to a star,
Keep your seat, and there you are.

Because she lived by that premise she was always accomplishing more than could be expected, and so were those who felt her inspiration.

Perhaps all the overachievers live by the same rule. In fact, it must be the reason the whole human race has gradually become more and more able to cope with new situations. When we prepare to develop, the results are gratifying. By drawing strength we want to use, we obtain it.

This is not the first century when people have felt that a better power than they knew was working through them. I suspect that never in history has this been better realized than it is today. We are familiar with the way religionists have always declared that there can be spiritual surprises, and of course all of us have always suspected that some secret caused the outstanding examples of genius. Yes, there is something beyond what we know that has made unusual personalities accomplish unusual successes. We feel grateful for the benefits left us by these blessed individuals and often wish we might know exactly how they operated.

Recently someone asked, "Wasn't it peculiar that Isaac Newton started to study the Bible in his later years, after he had depended upon mathematics until then?"

Someone else answered, "No doubt he was trying to find an explanation for his intellectual feats. It was the habit of his generation to look into the Bible for answers."

Others have glibly accorded credit to the "Good Lord" without trying to analyze further, but Newton was a man who wanted to figure out the how and why.

Nikola Tesla was another who was deeply pressed to interpret the unseen authority. One day during his youth, while he and a fellow student were observing a sunset, all at once he recognized a way to arrange great comforts for humanity. His biographer says:

Suddenly the animated figure of Tesla snapped into a rigid pose. He was gazing into the sun as if that incandescent ball had thrown him into a trance.

In that instant he conceived the alternating-current method that would prepare an amazing use for electricity.

"Isn't it sublime!" he exclaimed to his companion. "I have solved the problem. No more will men be slaves to hard tasks, for my motor will do the work of the world."

Later some of Tesla's studious friends claimed that he was "possessed of a great gift for the discovery of fundamental scientific principles."

During the next few years his patents numbered close to a hundred, and by now all his ideas have been put to work for the general public. Such a result of one man's skill has never been equaled. Regret has been expressed that Thomas Edison and George Westinghouse collected more financial good than Tesla himself enjoyed from his own diligence. But you may be sure that nothing could have surpassed the joy Tesla must have experienced in being used as a channel of divinity.

Was it Tesla's innocence—rather, his

clarity of perception—that enabled him to devise the means of worldwide communication? Because of his harnessing of the earth's impulses, all nations have become closer neighbors than ever could have been possible if he had not lived. Was there, indeed, a cosmic intention working through him? How is it that he became the instrument through which the natural tendencies were trained?

At any rate, certainly there was no accident in all this. It was too precise a procedure, too perfect a design to have been casual. Besides, it came at a time when it could meet an unspoken demand, for necessity had to result in satisfaction.

We others would willingly function as well, if only we could keep our mind susceptible; if only we could assume the required state of understanding. Does it take courage, or rare insight? Does it take more than the will to do? Perhaps we shall learn how to let divinity work through us if we stop doubting and forego modesty. It is not enough merely to stand back and marvel at the driving force of another, halting at what seems to be the margin of our own talent. We must extend that talent.

In all walks of life there are those who testify to an invisible power. George Washington Carver said: "When I touch that flower I am touching infinity. That little flower existed long before there were human beings on earth."

Frank C. Laubach, famed for his "each-one-teach-one" doctrine, spoke of the unseen: "I feel sure that our thoughts flow around the world even when we do not express them in words. If people realize that telepathy is a fact, we may yet attempt to make the world over by the sheer force of good thoughts."

Pico della Mirandola is quoted as having said in the fifteenth century, "The Great Artisan created man with an undetermined nature and then told him: you shall determine for yourself your own nature, in accordance with your free will."

Science has recently made possible the transplantation of parts for the body's preservation, and now it is far more important to contrive to renew the spirit. "Every cell in the body is being constantly replaced," says Wayne Cook, "so that we can improve our race immeasurably and eternally." What we need is the persistent preference of new horizons if we mean to do for the spirit what we know can be done for the body. We must envision and then shape the kind of world we want to inhabit and the kind of humanity we dream to be possible. All this requires an inner fortitude.

These days we have the biofeedback technique to lead the human family to effect healing by the very method that "new thought" has been advocating for the last one hundred years. We are now learning to control our thinking in order to introduce a conviction of health in all our livingness. At last in the laboratory psychologists are teaching volunteer "guinea pigs" to dictate the activity of their bodies.

Although Tesla's alternating current was formerly inconceivable, now it has become conventional. Once people had no technique for achieving the chosen bodily condition by means of visualization, and therefore they failed to take seriously their right to instruct in that direction. Now this control is within our normal grasp. Even as the surprising performance of electricity has endowed us with ease in daily tasks, now we have at our disposal the means of monitoring the brain by a tangible gadget and directing it to practice healing by silent decree. Soon we shall no longer need the equipment in a laboratory but shall insist that our body cells and nerves and muscles keep in perfect condition.

It is more and more necessary for us to accept what used to be the impossible. Let us dare! Not only in technology can we develop fertility of ideas; we can also enlarge the merely human capacities.

In the past it was considered praiseworthy to avoid experiments that risked failure, but now we boldly overcome any suspicion of fear and rise above reservations. Of course, an open mind is what generates enthusiasm for every further leap.

All that once seemed "nothing but hope"

is now known to be a phase of evolution, a precognition, in fact, the hardening of the determination to advance. It was first felt invisibly, then proved concretely. In modern industrialism reality has taken on a new aspect, and even educational systems now promote the use of thoughts in correcting physical distress. We make use of self-discipline, not only across the technical milieu, but also within behavior patterns. Our self-responsibility eliminates the hazards of ill health that heretofore were considered unrejectable because they were allowed to domineer.

As leaders of industry have expanded their operations, so too have invalids learned to assume responsibility for their renewed health by the prompting of biofeedback equipment and all that it will gradually imply. We now encourage the brain to amend an undesirable physique.

As I say, this is today's stage of evolution. We have been preparing for it without being able to define it. It has forced us through one confusion after another and now shows itself as wise practice, and even better prospects appear upon the horizon, ready to be seen when we are ready to see.

Certainly we have been guided by those individuals who followed each early gleam, whether or not they fathomed its importance. They were unable to deny the beckoning, even as the rest of us are today helpless to stop the progress. Every unguessed potentiality prompts us to recognize it. Vivid proofs have established positive thinking as the cure beyond question. Eventually we shall claim it automatically.

Every advance has resulted from the insight of one after another of those who ventured. The Oriental method of meditation has now been joined with Western practicality. Thus the combined human talents have brought us to the frontier where we are outgrowing the guessed-at limitations and are showing talents long untried.

Eventually (why not now?) we shall recognize the truth so well handed us by the sages of India:

Thought is a force, even as electricity and gravitation. The human mind is a spark of the almighty consciousness of God. Whatever your powerful mind believes very intensely will instantly come to pass.

This has an aroma of magic for those who have not tasted it, so let us counteract a suspicion of doubt by quoting a very practical man—the late Charles F. Kettering, who was vice-president of General Motors Corporation:

I think right now we have need for the greatest soul-setting endeavor on record. In other words, we have got to set our course—not a random course, not a wishful course, but a course that will get us to the destination we want. I think that, with ingenuity, faith, and determination, we can take this mysterious future, which isn't so very clear, and from it carve out anything that human imagination can think of that is worth carving out—that is, if it is for the benefit of the human family.

Perhaps—how should I know?—it was necessary for the human race to wade through the horror of repressions and brutalities before we could ever have reached today. From this outlook we can hardly pause to regret all that waste, while we travel to a point from which we can view the new goal. Even though we deplore the slowness of this attainment, still we are ready to rejoice at having come this far.

The claim that even "death can be cured" is a charming concept that looms beyond national barriers. Its simplicity opens our eyes to the prospect. We no longer have to allow circumstances to govern us—we can arrange circumstances of our choice.

Mankind is always saved, as often before proved, by a sturdy march toward a firmer aim, and here is our challenge. We are the ones who initiate each stage of evolution. Here we go!

Each of Us a Self-Healer

There is a secret wisdom in all of us, for we can guess that we are more than what we look like to strangers. Now and then we indulge in the luxury of contemplating the greatness of which we are a part. This is done by means of the practice that some call prayer, some call meditation, and others call the joy of daydreaming. These three or any one of them may enhance the dimension of a personality.

Unfortunately not everyone realizes that success, happiness, and health are due to the intelligent use of these gentle habits. Especially health—for most of us have been assured that health is governed by the physique itself.

But long ago Carl Jung explained, "Healing comes only from what leads the patient beyond himself and beyond his entanglement with the ego." This remark is quoted in one of Dr. Irving Oyle's books because in that physician's researches among several races of people he has discovered how true it is.

In fact, we do seem instinctively to seek protection from the ego when we want to attract better conditions of body and circumstance. We cannot do this when we remain under the influence of the personal will and the intellect, for these two talents are limited indeed. We have to find a better way.

Dr. Oyle reports a healing method that lies within the province of any thoughtful person, but he begs us: "Don't put me in the spook section, though! I'm just a family doctor trying to find out what it is that gets people well."

In order that we may control the behavior of our body, he advises that "visual technique be used in addition to standard medical techniques." His experiments with the power of the individual mind have shown him that as a healing device it is outstanding.

A doctor's relationship with a patient includes his own expectation that the ailing organism will absorb the medicine he administers. If his view is graphic enough it reestablishes normal health in the patient. Constructive thinking really does cause a cure whenever the patient exercises enough faith in the doctor's treatment to let go of the disease—which, for reasons of his own (known or unknown), the patient has unwittingly invited into his system. In his book Dr. Oyle italicizes the sentence: *"Whatever you put your trust in can be the precipitating agent for your cure."*

Regardless of any ritual employed, it is belief in its efficacy which brings about the desired result. It is important that the physician have complete confidence in his method and that he inspire the patient's confidence in it also. This sort of functioning in a devoted practitioner of previous days was responsible for the "bedside manner," seldom encountered today.

Dr. Oyle insists that the psyche's rate of vibration can (first) cause disease and (second) introduce healing—"directly proportionate to the patient's inner faith." And he adds that the stronger the faith, the better.

The modern biofeedback mechanism has been of excellent help in convincing the public that the mind can actually show its authority over all areas of the body. It proves even to doubters that the activity of internal organs (usually automatic) can be manipulated even as muscles can make the limbs move. A pen draws the evidence on a chart, when "mere" thought increases or decreases the body temperature or the rate of the heartbeat. This throws responsibility back upon the patient, where it has always belonged.

If the physician cannot immediately decide on how to treat a particular patient, he must at any rate do what he can to alleviate suffering, if only temporarily. Even when his procedure is no more than a gesture of cooperation, while he works with the patient he can invest his own faith. Often that is adequate.

When the patient is told to pay attention to any intuitive suggestion that occurs to him, before long he becomes aware of information that helps him start to contradict the hurt. With this beginning he soon gets the better of the unwelcome element.

Dr. Oyle declares that anyone can become a healer if he will spend fifteen minutes a day relaxing, counting backward from five to zero, seeing within the zero a picture of the patient's difficulty, then mentally replacing that picture in the zero with one that displays perfect health for the patient. This capacity of the mind can regulate material objects as well as living cells and tissues and organs, for we are performing in a world of crystallized thought. There is no solid flesh. Any idea of solidarity is imaginary. All is a composition of atomic particles that swing between states of existence and nonexistence.

Admitting that mind and matter are united, we weave between sensory impression and the way we see it, for the two are mutually creative. Every physical thing by its rate of vibration manifests in its own form.

Ideas as well as things are composed of energy, which can be tuned to different frequencies. That is the only way in which they differ.

Often the inner life flashes an image that thereupon generates evidence of neurotic or physical trouble. Just as frequently there may be beneficial flashes, but when an introspective person has assumed the custom of repressing these, they foment resistance which, in its turn, takes on the distressing form.

Dr. Oyle is accustomed to advising a patient to fancy himself in a comfortable place noticing his private thoughts. Usually in a short time the patient envisions a figure approaching, and he is supposed to ask, "Are you the one who gave me these symptoms? If so, why?"

Almost always it turns out that the patient can in this manner become silently apprised of whatever it was that he has been experiencing in his personal life to cause illness. When the body has conveyed this message to the brain, the patient cannot deny that it is up to him to get rid of his malaise. He can then formulate his own plan to make the proper correction.

Of course if the patient chooses *not* to recover, there is nothing the doctor can do to alter his course. It is quite possible to teach people how to maintain health and, when necessary, how to arrange a healing. But those who unconsciously prefer to escape life's burden can easily withstand this teaching. They follow the custom suitable to their temperaments, and very likely that to which their parents and grandparents succumbed. In such a case they refuse to cope with the deep advice. Only if they want to can they induce energy to flow from the unconscious domain to a form that can instruct them, and such a recognizable message must be heeded before its meaning can be of help.

It is obvious that a patient who submits to a regular program of meditation is one who has already backed away from the hidden inclination to be sick. It is therefore easy for him to release the tension (such as that which at times develops headaches). More dramatically, such a patient stops parading his anger at every hint of frustration. This alone immediately improves his personal relationships. Shortly afterward his physical endurance burgeons, with a churning up of greater energy followed by good work toward a goal.

One of Dr. Oyle's patients, following the examples called to her attention, decided to reject the verdict of cancer. She focused her thinking upon achieving the mental equivalent of normality, and during the next hospital examination her intention was confirmed by several kinds of tests. You may be sure that in this instance the patient must have grown out of whatever she had formerly been, for change is in line with all layers of existence, and her choice had to be for the better. Yes, causal relations do exist between the psyche and the body. Correspondingly, while the patient persists in his harmful pursuits, the ailment persists.

Symptoms are the means by which the psyche struggles against pressures that impede its essential work. Because the force of evolution must be served, it compels the body to overcome anything that would detain its progress. The body consequently suffers until the patient makes the required amendment in his thought pattern — or bows out.

Any person who claims to be ill is carelessly describing to himself the unwanted condition. This thought pattern is transmitted holographically and is planted in the contents of the body. To counteract this harm it is necessary to create a mental picture of the health you want. In that way you can accomplish a healing on the somatic level. Cosmic energy keeps its true balance when it is allowed to do so, whereas egocentric grumbling can only improvise and emphasize the disturbance. Children usually respond well to positive suggestion, perhaps because they are eager to get well, wanting to taste all the sweets of life and not assuming that the future may include defeats.

If you are worried or depressed, tell yourself how surely this is a matter of misapplied energy. Then breathe regularly, and note the immediate improvement. Practice letting energy race up and down your body until it feels encouraging. This gambit removes the body-blocks and enables you to entertain an anticipation of good. Right away the energy that has been wasted in the oppressive mood or the whining complaint becomes reversed and incites your self-congratulation. That is what we know as healing.

A quiet moment that you insist upon during a period of stress can be the commencement of a healing program. Remember that the constant flux of atomic energy has created the pattern of every internal organ and, in what from our viewpoint is called growth, has recreated it anew from instant to instant. This will help you to realize how amenable to your own demand every part of the body is.

The brain, like any computer, not only projects experience into the physical body within the environment, but it can also ameliorate that experience. Heretofore the physical was labeled as primary, while life was taken to be secondary and mind only derivative. Surely this conception was the best we had at the time, but now we see that it has had a destructive history. It is "only human" to apply the concept that seems best at any moment, but by now we have learned to accept new discoveries (such as the fact that the moon is attainable), so we can accept also the new knowledge that our bodies are continuous with the cosmos and with one another. At last we admit that what we think always affects others, and that what others think likewise affects us; that a mental state is contagious, and that the mind can select any certain experience at will.

Human beings are the means by which consciousness reproduces itself (as a fertilized egg does), and leap by leap the evolutionary process unfolds—from atom to civilization, from the first breath of life to the first hint of self-consciousness, on and on. Said Jung, "There is within the psyche a process that seeks its own goal independently of external factors."

Yes, it is mysterious. Shall we ever understand how our embryonic development initiates and directs its ordained end—if end there ever is? It forever changes all it works through and, says Dr. Oyle, the effort to remain in an earlier state is equivalent to the refusal of a fetus to be born. "To oppose the forces of nature invites destruction."

It takes courage for us to contemplate all this, but we are equal to any challenge. We can even take pride in the prospect, for we shall become more and more worthy of the opportunities that arise as we advance. Therefore, at any cost to the ego we must produce universal health and clear the way for our great destiny.

A Touch of Sublimity

Believe it or not, we really can "make our lives sublime," even though we may discount the sands of time. Within us is the power to associate ourself with what we like, and the mere proximity can make us match it.

Biologists tell us that all life forms exist in the aggregate, that particles adhere to one another, that a resulting organization of various components provides the environment in which they operate. We too are parts of the universe, and we too are activated within a complex of forces.

Aside from our biological apparatus, we rely upon a whole parcel called character to steer us through the ramifications of community living. Constantly we submit to a mental climate in which we can either flounder or rejoice at how well we are doing.

We are always reflecting the thoughts of others, whether we know it or not, and our selection of those others can mean our promotion or our deterrent. The fact that we are usually unconscious of the reason for the sway exerted upon us does not protect us from its influence. We are immune from the wrong only if we choose the right.

Therefore it is of practical importance to be surrounded by the best, and for this there is nothing better than exposure to notable predecessors. Ambitiously we seek the company of the admirable examples in history, and we move into a beneficial atmosphere merely by thinking of them. Our imagination allows us to absorb the collective condition of society while we court our highest potential.

We may as well celebrate our country's success by reading again the story of good old Ben Franklin. Much is known of him in general, but little is realized about what may benefit us in the elements that shone through his public service. Let us profit from an acquaintance with his personality, which attracted the love of his fellowmen while he helped to extend their welfare.

When Franklin was still a child, he discovered that he would not be popular if he allowed himself to become overbearing, and he vowed to develop "the Habit of expressing myself in terms of modest Diffidence, never using, when I advance any thing that may possibly be disputed, the words *Certainly, undoubtedly,* but rather saying *I conceive,* or *I apprehend a Thing to be so and so,* or *It appears to me.*"

So it was hardly by accident that he respected the opinions of his companions—and incidentally practiced the gentle art of persuasion. We may find it advantageous to contract this particular custom.

His wide reading from the time he was five years old made him revere books, but he chose them with an object in view: "to inform the Understanding rightly, and enable the Mind to frame great and noble ideas."

Such an aspiration brought about this conviction: "Without Freedom of Thought there can be no such Thing as Wisdom; and no such Thing as Publick Liberty without Freedom of Speech; which is the Right of every Man, as far as by it he does not hurt or controul the Right of another."

Doubtless we are willing to subscribe to this.

While still in his teens, Franklin regretted that women were not given the same educational opportunities that were available to men—although he himself had only two years of schooling. He also noticed that the writing of poetry was thought to be the province of England, and consequently was neglected by the colonists ("Upon which Consideration I have determined, when I meet with a Good Piece of New-England Poetry, to give it a suitable Encomium in order to encourage the Author to go on.").

And later he described, with enviable restraint, the faulty logic in race prejudice:

"If an Indian injured me, does it follow that I may revenge that injury on all Indians?

The only Crime of these poor Wretches seems to have been, that they had a reddish brown Skin and Black Hair; and some People of that Sort, it seems had murdered some of our Relations. If it be right to kill Men for such a Reason, then, should any man, with a freckled Face and red Hair, kill a wife or Child of mine, it would be right for me to revenge it, by killing all the freckled red-haired Men, Women, and Children I could afterwards any where meet with."

In another instance, Franklin showed not only intelligence but especially compassion such as can well be appreciated in the present period of the senior citizen. His favorite sister had written him that she was planning to transplant their older half-sister to a retirement home, and he replied:

"As having their own way is one of the greatest Comforts of Life, to old People, I think their Friends should endeavor to accommodate them in that, as well as in any thing else. When they have long liv'd in a House, it becomes natural to them, they are almost as closely connected with it as the

Tortoise with his Shell, they die if you tear them out of it. Old Folks and old Trees, if you remove them, 'tis ten to one that you kill them. So let our good old Sister be no more importun'd on that head. We are growing old fast ourselves, and shall expect the same kind of Indulgencies. If we give them, we shall have a Right to receive them in our Turn."

One Englishman advised Franklin that he was wise to test electricity "from your own nature instead of studying others: for then you will certainly find many other things which have been hidden to natural philosophers throughout the course of centuries." That course Franklin continued to follow, and his reports were always written from firsthand observation in "a close, naked, natural way of speaking." He repeatedly gave credit to any from whom he was able to take hints that helped his own progress, showing appreciation and generosity too.

Because some of his laboratory work encroached upon unknown realms, he said, "I feel a Want of Terms," and he had to invent descriptions. Many of the electric terms that he initiated are still in use: *armature, battery, condenser, positive, negative,* etc. His curiosity led him to such outstanding accomplishments in this area that a history of science was entitled "Franklin and Newton." Insofar as we can, we ought to emulate his diligence and originality.

One commentator summarized: "It is not easy to say whether we are most pleased with the simplicity and perspicuity with which Franklin proposes every hypothesis of his own, or the noble frankness with which he relates his mistakes, when they are corrected by subsequent experiments." And Franklin himself exclaimed, "How many pretty systems do we build, which we soon find ourselves oblig'd to destroy!"

We still speak well of anyone who acknowledges a misstep.

It has been said that Franklin had a vision of the future, but it is more likely that he shaped the future as he wished it to become. His persistence continually kept open the door to his expectations. He was willing to persevere for any necessary length of time, never giving way to the possibility of failure—the sort of attitude that is familiar today when positive thinking is widely recommended.

Yet he was equally vigilant to show himself agreeable to the interests of others. This latter trait became evident after the start of the Revolutionary War when he represented the colonies in France, seemingly having nothing with which to barter. There is a fine distinction between subservience and cooperation, between entreaty and tact. He exercised dignity while encouraging intimacy with the wily king's minister, during the long years when he was consulted only in official secrecy. These negotiations were conducted with a mixture of integrity and discretion, while he governed his every word and move. It could not hurt us to learn from his control.

Always avoiding vanity and haste, he graciously yielded to the French official's plans without relaxing his urgent efforts on behalf of the colonies. He also collected funds and supplies and armaments and recruits for George Washington's army while, despite distance of time and ocean, he laid the cornerstone of the new country's diplomacy. When his quiet handling of matters culminated in the Treaty of Paris (which validated France's alliance with and support of the Revolutionists), at last the United States was enrolled as a member of the world of nations.

As one historian expressed it, that treaty "produced the greatest blessings to both contracting parties" and "the greatest benefit to civilisation as a whole." No wonder Franklin was praised for his "sanity and clear sense." A diplomat's venture, even in the modern world, depends upon skill in candid discussion, plus wisdom to retain balance between opponents.

When at last Franklin was presented at the French court, he accepted the long-postponed honor without any hint that he may have expected it earlier. He was without recrimination, for he thoroughly knew the reason for the delay. The treaty had in effect created the new nation, and only then, according to international usage, was he entitled to equal status with the French signatories. Had he been less prudent in any of the crises during his stay in Paris, the full value of his project could have been reduced or possibly annulled. What patience!

Franklin's intentions became justified only by means of a combination of his talents, but his conspicuous virtue was forbearance.

We are tempted to ask: "How did he get that way? He taught himself? Well, what was there about him that made it possible for him to teach himself? Did he have this aptitude at birth? If so, where did he get it?"

We have asked such questions about other highly competent persons, and the fact is that we do not know the answer. We are still mystified. Sometimes Franklin spoke casually of the continuity of life after this stage, and he may have guessed that this one had grown out of a previous one, during which he prepared for his role here. Did he know that he came into this life with an accumulation of knowledge which he was always increasing for the sake of lives yet to be lived?

That may have been only a hazy suggestion in his thoughts. However, he seems quite definitely (in his unorthodox manner) to have been aware of a higher Supervisor, and this may have emphasized his confidence. Certainly it was some such impersonal view that fortified his purpose. Did it also assure him that the Supervisor's wisdom was available on demand? Surely he, like the rest of us, had access to daily guidance in whatever extent he was able to receive it. At any rate, he strove consistently for an open mind and may have reached understanding for that reason.

All this is speculation, yet the details of his biography suggest it.

Now, this is the point: when you and I survey our own characteristics, we admit that we could not admire Franklin as we do had we no similar tendencies. The great majority of men and women who know his name approve of him. Perhaps we can even find traces that we have inherited some of his qualities.

Thereupon our responsibility is aroused. In

the chain of influences, person to person, long before Franklin lived and ever after, examples of excellence are being transmitted. It is startling to realize that we too swing our weight upon the lives of others. In leaving the flavor of all we are, wherever we go, are we positive that it will infuse heroism in those who follow? Are we satisfied that, within the complex in which we operate as particles, we are investing our bit toward the improvement of the human race?

How good we should feel if we could be sure of this! Anyway, we know that the fabric of humanity is strengthened by every personal relationship that is nurtured in the cradle of courtesy. Circumstances testify that to esteem an adversary is to transform him into a friend, and any test of this principle proclaims its feasibility.

In every transaction, then, let us inspire reciprocal confidence in order that we may gradually erect the utopia that instinctively we know to be our natural home.

The Call of the Future

Whenever I come up with what looks like a new idea, I understand exactly how Little Jack Horner felt when he pulled out a plum. Later I am likely to learn that the "new" idea has already been known by others. At any rate, Little Jack Horner and I have both known an instant of triumph, leaning in our own way toward a desired climax. Our flash of insight has been one step on the climb.

One day I asked myself: "Is it true that only living things are in the onward parade? Or do unliving things float on the same stream toward a culmination?"

I had read Pierre Teilhard de Chardin's claim that consciousness had been born to raise the element of life out of matter, but even then I continued to think that matter and livingness were opposed. I knew that awareness of a future attracts us to our likes: there is more joy in a budding friendship that promises long-lasting satisfaction than in a passing contact. But does a nonliving mountain, for instance, expect the enrichment of soil to result from its crumbling?

Amid the present-day proliferation of psychic news, every least evidence of the expanding powers of the human mind and spirit wins our surprised attention. But there is special reason for us to regard with wonder a startling breakthrough that defines the value of the material in connection with the spiritual. We no longer speak of two worlds, one physical and the other abstract. It is now known that together they make one world.

Four hundred years ago Galileo was persecuted for saying that the earth was not the center of the universe, because that thought jogged men painfully out of their egocentricity, and they resisted. In our own time Albert

Einstein spoke of the gap that is closed after the brain has gone as far as it can go—how a new order of intelligence inexplicably assumes a farther beachhead. What was he talking about if not the advance of the psychic range?

It has long been said that a few seconds after a new thought enters the brain, the chemical composition of the whole body is changed. Then in all likelihood each particle of the universe has an influence upon every other particle, constantly increasing the interaction of all particles. Every atom, as an organized whole, responds to direction into a higher form. Parallel to the *without* is always a *within,* spontaneously unfolding matter toward spirit.

Thus we are all pressing on "toward the goal for the prize of the upward call of God." In fact, although we are mostly unconscious that it is so, we have secret access to this truth, perhaps by what is called extrasensory perception. And now we are told that ESP is not "extra" at all, only an ordinary perception at an ultrahigh frequency. Perhaps it is an association impinging upon one or another of the five familiar senses. Certainly it is within our normal apparatus, like the overflow of undercurrent memory. Some persons defend themselves against encroachment by strangers, and they fail to experience any *psi* reaction at all; others are naturally receptive to impressions.

None of us ever has any special experience until after he has become amenable to it. As Kahlil Gibran says, "No man can reveal to you aught but that which already lies half asleep in the dawning of your knowledge." When we seek a congenial environment and sympathetic companions, we are ready to imbibe the nectar of an enlarged potential.

My friend Marybeth tells me: "It isn't supernatural at all when people get hunches. I insist it is perfectly natural. While I'm playing Yahtze I get an electric flutter in my solar plexus just when the number coming up is the one I need in order to win. I don't try to control the dice—of course not! I simply happen to know, before I see the number, that it's going to be what I want."

You can be sure that this principle is noticeable whenever the circumstances are comparable, but we must shape the circumstances to suit us. When a healing is needed, or when we have a particular job to do, we must condition ourself to effect it. The not-for-self willingness to welcome a certain outcome provides the technique that enables us to acquire prosperity, or bounding health, or desirable relationships. What we call prayer can place us in the mood to accomplish all this (correction: to receive all this).

The marvel is that human beings often take hold of something unseen and unproven, while yet far from knowing how it could possibly be.

Long before we knew about molecules, we were proclaiming the wonder of the firmament. Long before we knew how to outwit microbes, we were declaring that mind and health are related. Has each discovered fact been preordained? Is this why certain events are foreseen? Was Darwin's natural selection indeed left to itself, or was it a purposeful system that sent out tentacles to grasp something waiting to be grasped?

Well, this concept is now justified by a series of laboratory explorations that convince even the skeptic. At last we recognize a Force in the inanimate that has always followed an intention to reach the animate as its inescapable destination.

Early in this century Sir Jagadis Chandra Bose, working in India, found "points of contact emerging between the living and the nonliving." He could not "draw a line and say that here the physical phenomenon ends and here the physiological begins," but he reported on the uninterrupted extension from the first hint of creation toward what we now behold. His announcement of a similarity between reactions of metals and plants and animal tissues was hardly accepted while his methods relied upon delicate instruments not available to others.

We were amused when the poet Robinson Jeffers revered life in rocks, and since his death we have been astounded by the information that plants are influenced by human thoughts. But now Bose's work makes us smile at our earlier supposition that human beings are alone in importance, that minerals and vegetation are here only to serve us. We are growing out of that mistake and are realizing that, rather, it is we who are resulting from them.

There is a more recent proof that a tiny ingredient of a tiny particle within a tiny cell is kindred to the fullness of the universe and is itself summoned toward immortality. Such proof has won a Nobel prize for Dr. Albert Szent-Gyoergyi. This Hungarian chemist traced the process through the inanimate into plant life, and hence into the variety of animal life. Thus he confirms in the test tube the pronouncement that *all is one,* to an extent never before remotely supposed.

"We probably all feel," he says, "that there is some basic difference between the living and the nonliving, while as scientists we cannot believe that the laws of the universe should lose their validity at the surface of our skin."

Once it was said that the universe represented either random motion or design, and the human brain took a long time to admit that design was possible despite the myths that primitives concocted to encourage that view. We simply could not cope with a truth that was too grand to be true. But now there is undeniable evidence against the casual notion, for nature's steady march belies it in the chain of electrons that extends into the molecule.

"How wonderfully subtle and complex is the structure of even a simple molecule . . . a very specific individuality!" says Szent-Gyoergyi. The flow of electrons linking the molecules is "a clear-cut example of life being kept in the living condition by life itself, kept by work in good working order."

In a definite current molecules combine until a cell is reproduced by self-division, causing exact duplication although it also includes the potential to evolve. Thereupon differentiation appears in the program as an unyielding purpose. The cell is intuitively regulated to attract other cells into further intricacies, seeming to murmur, "We must go forward to the things which are before."

When sex is finally introduced, it is not for the purpose of reproduction as all former movement was. Instead, it is to avoid duplication—to initiate a mixture of heredities. Each new existence no longer resembles its forbears, "though the basic rules remain unchanged."

Consciousness contains the power to expand its own equipment. Its scheme actually resides in the molecules that precede living matter as they perform their part in evolution by constituting the support without which there could be no new launchings.

The living organism ingests food which turns into chemical energy, which causes activity, which instigates muscle, which. . . .

On and on!

The inner insistence operates further and further toward future patterns. This, in the poet's language, is "persistent aspiration."

You have heard of the person who tried to encourage a backwoodsman to do more than wait to die: "Why, Zeke, the world has a job for you to do!" Zeke replied, "Well, I ain't a-gonna do it."

For Zeke, evolution was at an end. Being without a philosophy, he succumbed to despair. If he had known that part of his composition was preparing for immortality, he could have been redeemed. He did not know that he was suffering simply from unbelief.

But the rest of us avidly contribute to the tantalizing panorama of things to come. Given time, this very race of men and women will reach unbelievable glory, but separately we cannot go far. Only shoulder to shoulder can we fulfill the unspoken expectation that draws us irresistibly.

We do not know when empathy entered into the procession, but nowadays we can no longer ignore the feeling of compassion for others: the success of others means our own success. Together we are future-oriented because the primeval core carries this imperative. It magnetizes us notwithstanding the reluctance that may at times be coddled by our ignorance. Within each of us is a response to the call of the future. And so we adjust our attitudes on the positive side, developing the quality of our skills and focusing them judiciously.

"Vision and reality are intertwined," says Liz Campbell of the Association for Humanistic Psychology. "They shape each other. What we think is possible, or probable, influences what happens. . . . Limited visions restrict what can happen, while our limited experience shrinks our vision."

In this circular fashion we acknowledge the power of the human psyche, which has descended from further back than we can guess. Of course Goethe said this in verse, but that used to be recited only in a manner to tease us into trying harder. Now it is soberly regarded as a plan by which our personal affairs may be navigated.

"I think it is not improbable," said Justice Oliver Wendell Holmes, with the caution native to any follower of the legal profession, "that man may have cosmic destinies that he does not understand."

True—he does not understand. "It does not yet appear what we shall be." But we do realize that we are being drawn relentlessly Godward. On the way, in a moment of ecstasy, Little Jack Horner and I can pluck a plum from the immensity around us.

How Wonderful We Are!

Positively, we are unique, worthy of congratulation if only because we are members of the human race. We must never discount the fact that in merely being human we are specimens of grandeur. We don't always meet our highest demand, but this we realize, and we try harder. With all our faults (and we are smart enough to know we do have some of them), we still have remarkable valor.

This is, of course, because we are reflections of an overall wisdom that we hardly pretend to understand. No mortal mind could short-circuit the guidance of the Intelligence that has created what we are with all our potential. In fact, whenever one of us does get off the track, as a result of willfulness, circumstances steer us back before we have been able to wreak permanent damage. We can always return to the safer road.

Do you realize that for centuries we have been constantly solving problems as rapidly as they have arisen? At no time in history has there been any stoppage of mankind's forward reach, and at this moment there is less single worry than there is worry about the race as a block. Is that an improvement? You may be sure it is. All "persons of consequence" you meet soon show themselves to be active in one or another social movement. The happiest people you know are those whose private experience is encompassed by public interest. And, of course, even you and I are concerned about the Earth and all those who dwell upon it. We are equal passengers on a relentless journey, and only what is salutary for all can be of advantage to us.

These days we often hear the complaint that the riches of the globe may soon be dissipated. One daring soul even gave a date for this catastrophe, such as, say, 2025. But just as frequently we hear the answer that comes from the well-modulated voice of a nameless speaker: "Doomsayers fail to take into consideration the ingenuity of man."

Precisely. That reminder cheers us because it is the promise that bounty will prevail. Human nature is mysterious, but it has a basis in both spiritual and physical aspects. Therefore we seek a purpose beyond our own sakes, and it is esteem for our fellow travelers that helps us cherish the human condition. There is always work in progress that will protect our good in the years to come.

In my childhood I knew that the family rule was to avoid selfishness, but I silently argued, "How can I, when this me is the place where I start?" Nevertheless, gradually even I became imbued with sympathy for the others around me. Conscience tells us that it is wrong to remain self-centered, and we can never rest until we overcome that tendency. We always want to transcend the little self. The supra-personal transfigures the self-centered creature into an instrument of giving.

The first proud glow in a child comes when he has found a way to mend his friend's broken wagon, or when he has caught his little sister as she was falling. Through every stage of satisfaction, from the small to the patriotic, there is a stream of reward beyond the practical explanation. Now that the world view is stretching the possibilities of help to all persons, there will be more grandeur experienced in each heart.

Today we benefit hourly from the discoveries of individuals of the past, and the least of us enjoys improvements that a century ago were outside the realm of imagination. All that electricity affords, all that agriculture has gained, all that rapid communication endows, and all that public health has instigated have enhanced our prospects. Even now certain scholars are experimenting with methods to protect the populace from starvation in the event we squander our present resources. Devices as yet uncrystallized will maintain our favorite projects and enlarge our capacities, and many subtle facilities will prepare the further advance of civilization over anything we are acquainted with now. There will be, you can readily believe, both systematic progress and the increased gratification of art.

Plato characterized the artist as one who gives birth to some new reality, and one modern scientist asks, "What if our logic and science derive from art forms and are dependent upon them, rather than art being merely a decoration for our work?" Of course both are true.

When the biologist tells us what he considers to be fact, he may be spreading his art upon us. In National Wildlife Magazine for June 1976, we read of the

> ... *clear, high chirping produced by the insect rubbing together the file and the scraper located on its fore wings. When air temperatures rise, the cricket's bodily processes speed up. In fact, the snowy tree cricket's response to rising temperature is so attuned that you can estimate the temperature by counting the*

chirps it utters in 15 seconds and adding 39. For instance, 35 chirps in 15 seconds equals 74 degrees Fahrenheit.

Now, this sounds very factual indeed, and yet it is an observation close to art. It is a description from the human viewpoint, and we make no effort to verify it from the insect's own claim. We can call it a scientific explanation and nod in satisfaction. The hidden artist in each of us is appeased, for we accept this verdict as a shared label of truth, and our relationship with one another is more firm.

When someone exclaims, "Isn't it wonderful that we understand the cricket?" Someone else may return wryly, "It would be more wonderful if we could understand the cricket as well as we think we do."

The ego is always trying to become more and more objective.

We frequently read something that enlightens us, and we are likely to murmur, "I didn't know that!" in surprise that there is anything at all still foreign to us. Often our life is enriched, or our path changed, by someone else's casual remark. Truth to tell, we meander through life collecting daily knowledge and garnishing it with accidental contributions from people we meet (or pass without recognition). When we realize this, we may personally be careful to spread only benefits.

Each of us may feel inventive enough to perform a service by talking about what we consider an eye-opener, and when we hear the pronouncements of others we accept them as original. For instance, Rollo May, a master at giving instructions, has sincerely recommended that we should use the power of mental decisions to improve character. Because of his advice we are better able to select thoughts that can lead us into improved activity of both mind and body.

But after he had been teaching in this vein for years, one day it dawned upon him that the Dutch philosopher, Baruch Spinoza, who died in 1677, had taught his own students, "Fasten your attention upon some virtue that you want to acquire, and in time it will have become a part of your personal equipment."

Then Rollo May realized that his own "new" idea had been tracing the trail made long ago by the footsteps of others. How many of us are leaving a similar effect without even knowing it?

Jacob Bronowsky, in his brilliant TV series on "The Ascent of Man," commented on the way the human mind has developed. And, strangely enough, after giving us this report, he backstepped to the point of deploring the current use of Zen and what is called ESP. Evidently he fell short of seeing that both these methods are only "aiding and abetting" the very growth possibilities that he was admiring. It is by definite experiment that ideas are transmuted from one stage of usefulness to another. Bronowsky's own mental sharpness was no doubt developed through similar private trials by earlier generations, though he had come by his own understanding so naturally that he did not credit such approaches.

The distinction of the human animal is its effort to use evolution for its own purpose (no matter how it happens that such purpose has been impregnated within his genes). We keep fashioning a future to match our best desire, even while "the future becomes no longer what it used to be." Our habit of inserting our own will into everything we encounter—the leveling of a mountain or the filling of a pond—is all the more proved by recurring challenges to plot new means of coping.

We are human enough to value fidelity: "While life lasts I swear to you. . . ." Contrarily, we are also human enough to combat conformism with comments such as, "New situations require new remedies." We are never satisfied to be as we are. We strive to become something more, and choices are always enticing us. We are forced to assume whatever courage we need, to satisfy demands as they are made upon us, and we thrill to necessity.

We never work alone even when we believe we do, but we proceed by rubbing elbows with others, by encouraging and receiving encouragement. We seek those who let us confide our miseries and those who praise our conquests. Blissfully unaware of how such a practice can affect us, we are yet always contriving to mingle, to corroborate, or to dispute, more than ever when we suspect that such contact may possibly have its dangers. We ask, "What is around the corner?" and we dare one another to take one further step.

When we have not words enough to describe our constant extension, we use symbols, and in this way, innocently enough, we enter into the art world. Thus, while partaking in a creative act, our personal curiosity applies another layer upon the social structure. We may believe that we are alone, while doing this, or we may feel a group pressure, but we could never carry on in a vacuum. We are really being swept along in silent or acknowledged unity. We are integers in an eternal puzzle. All we can do is to select our companions so as to move in the ambience we prefer.

The wonder is that we are always entertaining concepts for improvement. We are automatically cooperating with divine direction, or resting upon it, or drawing strength from it, or engaging its design with every claim we make to originality.

We can never fail to flow with the force of universal consciousness, even when we decide to rebel, for such a decision is itself part of the force with which we are flowing. The safety of our fellow human beings is our own safety, and there can be no lasting conflict, because all effort has its birth in the Source.

Not one of us is a maverick; we all wear the everlasting brand of mankind. In every act we move straight toward a culmination that we feel drawing us, though we cannot name it. Almost every person has felt what we call destiny outlining the path to follow in a profession or other activity. When we are old we can look back and say, "In youth I felt it was important to do this very thing." Musicians or politicians or teachers or builders can never remember a time when their true vocation was not beckoning them in one form or another. Mozart is our great example, Churchill another, and among the countless unknown there are still the beginnings that could never be denied.

Not too long ago only a small percentage of people ever went through all eight grades of what used to be called "grammar school." When a graduation class reached its goal there was speculation among the neighbors as to how many of the pupils might be able to enter high school. There was shaking of heads: "Too bad, but very few will ever reach the fourth year at high school."

Now it is quite usual for boys and girls to graduate from high school, and even the doubt about their being qualified to enter college has been discarded. Arrangements have been made to meet the requirements of the various students. In fact, many hundreds of colleges have been inaugurated in various sections of the country in response to the public need. Many such colleges are newly founded during my own lifetime, necessitated by a whole new layer of accommodation. It has become quite usual for older people to resort to college after raising families, whereas for generations only the young were ever admitted to classwork. The spread among the population and the community arrangements to meet the necessity for higher education make up the characteristic of this new age.

All this has encouraged countless adult organizations throughout the country to provide their newly enrolled members with undreamed of educational opportunities. Conferences, symposia, congresses, summer sessions, "celebrations," and many other events attract congregations of adult students in beautiful country places or on college campuses, for the discussion of special psychologies, often under the tutelage of famous university professors.

What an advance from the last century's social functions when men and women paraded for no other purpose than to exhibit expensive costumes and snobbish preferences! People are no longer satisfied to assemble merely for the sake of acquaintanceship—they now seek common interests in the intellectual field. They invest their time and money in group study, often without any recognition, such as college credit, actually for the choice of mental pursuits.

At present this is such a widespread custom that it is lifting the general intelligence noticeably, and one of the offshoots (overwhelming any pretense at mere sociability by the exchange of developing ideas) is the advance in the education of children. Of all the human plans that have improved the mortal lot, the angle that educators are now stressing may be one of the most important.

Right now there is wide encouragement for the natural psychic development of children instead of insistence that it be stamped out of them before puberty. Once they were taught to say a circumscribed prayer but ridiculed if they perceived any answer to it. Now they are not ridiculed if they believe they receive an inner response to their cogitations. Their instinctive talent to judge between alternatives can help them as they reach adulthood to establish sturdier public health physically and mentally. Seeing the Truth as against blind convention can uncover for the rising generation the negative emotional patterns that the average child previously was forced to accept from his parents' subconscious. Once they were not allowed to analyze the family influence and protect themselves from it, but now they tap their own soul and, through an inner message, correct the harmful parental implications before they accumulate enough crust to hurt.

Children are at last freed from a program unwisely contracted by parents who themselves were crippled by their private histories. No longer do children submit to the hidden disturbances that burden their parents. Ripe with intuition they now appraise each situation and become enabled to relieve the parents and also to claim their own liberation. Thus a child under the new educational method prevents his moral disfigurement and, incidentally, releases the parents from their own outdated contagions.

When young Allen walked into the house with his trousers torn, his mother started to scold, and because he had been taught to evaluate such a mood he said offhandedly, "Don't worry about it, Mother. These pants will soon be too small for me anyway."

She bridled, a new view of the matter before her mind's eye, but still she had to rationalize, so she insisted, "All the more reason to take care of them while they still fit you."

By that time her anger had thinned, and the boy went up to his room whistling. He had arrived at his commonsense estimate instead of being steamrollered by a parent's peculiar complex (the probable cause of which may have been a sheaf of grievances never uncovered). In interpreting the incident with perspective he had at the same time recharged himself.

The new handling of the rising generation may turn out to be one of the most important methods yet devised to advance the human race. The very self-centeredness with which separately we began has conducted us to a point where we see a private hurt as a public need, and we are pressed to solve it for the general good without the lonely cringing that heretofore governed us. The modern psychology which recommends continual consultation—intimate communication among large groups—is opening new doors. Our goal, the good of the whole, is today's lesson, and it is preparing us for a grander lesson tomorrow.

We shall continue to search for and to act upon the spiritual principle, because to do so is our nature. And that is the secret that proves how wonderful we are.

The Marriage of Mind and Matter

Just because many of us realize that mental attitude can color whatever it is we think we see, we tend to place importance in the thought that underlies the obvious. At the same time we are likely to doubt ourself when we are accused of romanticizing. This must be the reason that we show particular interest when a recognized authority in science confirms our apologetic suspicion about the fundamental truth of things.

The erudite author Arthur Koestler is on our side. He has had personal experience with insight and other phases of metaphysics. He makes us feel justified in our airy preoccupation when he quotes Sir Arthur Eddington to this effect: the deeper we delve into the problems of science, the more we feel convinced that the universe is composed of mind-stuff. Eddington, of course, knew whereof he spoke.

Decades ago the same physicist said, "The frank realization that physical science is concerned with a world of shadows is one of the most significant of recent advances."

In his youth Sir James Jeans (bracketed along with Arthur Eddington as open-minded) spoke of the stream of man's knowledge as "heading toward a nonmechanical reality; the universe begins to look more like a great thought than like a great machine."

All right. Then when we say that prayer is answered or that telepathy works, we are merely mentioning our own choice of elements within that world of shadows sworn to by laboratory technicians themselves.

Again, we can take comfort in knowing that the will-o'-the-wisp called "whim" is characteristic not only of the human mind. Other things in the universe evidence the same caprice. From our viewpoint, for instance, the electron has neither form nor stability; it remains neither in motion nor at rest. Can anything be more quixotic than that? Certainly it resembles the capacity of mind-stuff. If the electron is an example of actuality, perhaps many of the things we think we know can be contradicted within the length of a wink. Both action and nonaction become more difficult to believe than ghost stories of antiquity.

We laymen are obliged to accept all the abstruse calculations by which scientists prove reality. And, surely, who are we to question an opinion about the mysterious cyclotron? Though others fault our hunches, we dare not name their hard-earned discoveries conjectures. Within their private discipline they can check on one another's pronouncements and support one another's claims by their own secret code. Being outside their clique, we are powerless to argue—but they assume the right to argue against our faith in affirmations.

If the two views meet to the extent that

both operate in a world of shadows, where all is composed of mind-stuff, then mind and matter can no longer be called opposing aspects. There is so much subtlety in nature that we certainly cannot rely upon such simplicity as the separation of those two cousins.

Of course we know that mind can receive information emanating from persons and things without the intervention of matter. This means that not all interactions are manifestations of material instruments. On the other hand, nonmaterial functions are frequently described by the basic equations of quantum physics. But non-things of quantum physics are elusive; consequently nowadays we have to practice thinking outside the conventional space-time slot if we expect to understand what we are talking about. Nonsubstantial consciousness belongs to life as surely as squash and pickles do.

Previous disclosures in physics had relevance only when they pertained to substance. But at present nonsubstantial qualities are known to dominate. Believe it or not, by now we have learned that matter dissolves into energy and energy into amorphous configurations. Here we are—up against the unthinkable!

So mass is transformed into energy and energy into mass. How shall we believe that light (which is without mass) by flying past an atomic nucleus becomes converted into an electron and an anti-electron, both of which possess mass? Everything we have called palpable must now be transferred to the realm of illusion, and *vice versa*.

At first glance it may seem illogical that several of the founders of the London Psychic Society in the nineteenth century were physicists of high caliber. But it turns out that the incidents they observed in physics had a strong connection with the assertions of psychics. Their laboratory experiments produced knowledge too graphic for denial, and they considered it urgent to group the two studies if they hoped for clarification.

When vibrations, for instance, were recorded, it was necessary to determine what it was that vibrated. Some matter behaved like waves and some like particles, but why or when? And were there any self-consistent rules to personal experiences that occurred without occupying space? F. W. H. Myers and other scholars wanted to find the answers to such questions, and therefore they risked ridicule by applying tests to psychic phenomena.

Practical or not, we can no longer ignore what seems to be "imaginary." Everything known is of whatsoever character it is, despite the limitation of our means of measuring it. For all we know, what we have seen as elementary may be conglomerate when its surrealistic essence is examined.

Koestler encourages us to regard that unknown thing called a neutrino. It has no physical attributes, not even a magnetic field. Someone announced its existence twenty-five years before there was equipment to observe it. Now it is known to be not subject to gravity, even free of interference by fragments that may be within its general proximity at any time. It travels at a greater velocity than light does, and it is wily enough to pierce through solid substance.

Said the astronomer V. A. Firsoff: "The universe as seen by a neutrino would wear a very unfamiliar look. Our earth and the other planets simply would not be there," because the neutrino drives through them without knowing they are in its path. It exists in its own kind of space and time, obeying its own laws which pertain to nothing else we know.

The neutrino could never have been detected if it had not occasionally come into collision with its match—a chance of one in many millions, due to its smallness and the distance it usually keeps from all its relations. Its quasi-ethereal traits make it seem only a fantasy. Somebody postulated that it may be the missing link between matter and mind, but before we could ratify this we would have to be sure of the peculiar properties of both matter and mind.

Koestler comments, "Penetration to this depth below the world of appearance is one of the greatest triumphs of human ingenuity."

This is the point: present-day wisdom requires that we respect impossibles in the substance sphere—black holes in space, for instance. We must be hospitable to the idea that there are sounds of a frequency beyond our ability to intercept, shocks to which we are impervious, unknown forces that coerce our conduct. While we are living within our skin, pondering on our surroundings without being able to visualize agencies that sway us, there is no longer any excuse for us to give credence only to physical effects.

At last we admit that trans-psychic realities touch upon nuclear products, that space-time is paradoxical. We have even ascertained that intangible but influential particles rush backward in time. Is this an explanation of precognition? That is, if a "future" episode moves backward in time, it encounters our present awareness. Then how does that event get back to its appointed "future" niche so as to clash conveniently with our mental reception at its originally ordained moment? Perhaps it is always in its own spot, now and then flashing only its likeness across space to be seen at a distance by those susceptible to mirages.

We know that telescopes and microscopes enable us to see what our eyes alone could never see. We also know that many scientific propositions pertain to material objects never seen but whose effects are clear. Acknowledging all this in physics, we can never again gainsay what unbelievers label aberrations.

The journalist William Allen White, years after the night when he saw "the little people" dancing beneath a tree outside his bedroom window, said he must have been crazy—but he knew he wasn't, his autobiography adds. His conviction is as trustworthy as many conclusions reached in astronomy. That the sun was the center of the universe was accepted as fact for centuries until proved erroneous. That fairies cannot be seen dancing in the grass has been accepted as fact, but that does not mean it is true.

When Bill White was keyed up with anticipation of his worldly success about to start the next day, he may well have seen something for which at any other time he would not have had the proper modulation of response. The vision persisted for several minutes, while he accused himself of delusion and tried to combat it. Then the joyous scene gradually faded out of the range of his eyes while he stared. There is plenty of reason for us to credit his description of what he thought he saw.

Each of us acts as a cosmic resonator, united with all the components of universal harmony. Schopenhauer decided, "Everything is interrelated and mutually attuned," and Whitehead emphasized, "Any local agitation shakes the whole universe." In other words, we are entangled together "for the duration."

You see how exciting life can be when we meet squarely with questions begging for solution. The absence of answers is all the more stimulating. We are learning that it is essential to govern our thoughts and words and actions in order to fashion the life we choose, instead of succumbing to automatism in the general whirl. Inasmuch as the universe is mind-stuff, let us empower our own share of that stuff to erect situations in line with our calculated preference.

To direct our tendencies, we must select the vibrations we exude upon others as well as those to which we submit. When we intend to gravitate toward a higher status, we radiate loving-kindness and shun inferences of hostility. The price of vigilance in this exercise is not too high, for the goal is increasingly rewarding.

In a recent magazine article Marcus Bach wrote about the "new man" whom he calls *Homo sapiens subliminalis*. "As far as he is concerned, deeds and actions are no longer valid merely on the basis of hope of reward or recognition. They are metapersonal, transcending thought of self . . . not necessarily because of any ego-effacing attitude but because he knows that power lies above the personal."

Others too believe that the improved race of man, resulting from purpose, is already in evidence in the form of the next higher stage of evolution. C. S. Lewis explains this rather prudently: "Already the new men are dotted here and there all over the earth. Every now and then one meets them. Their very voices and faces are different from ours. When you have recognized one of them, you will recognize the next one much more easily. And I strongly suspect (but how should I know?) that they recognize one another immediately and infallibly, across every barrier of color, sex, class, age, and even of creeds. In that way, to become holy is rather like joining a secret society."

This may be only a dream not yet implemented with enough reliable instances. But it gives a clue. As the athlete develops muscle, so we can train our inherent talents by daily taking advantage of the chance to use mindstuff for a lofty purpose. Why wait for biological evolution to enhance the race? We now take the initiative.

By drawing upon imperceptible elements such as love, we are able to invest in the dreamed-of promotion instead of accumulating back accounts. Money is at the mercy of international maneuvering, useless in crisis. But in a world where all creatures exchange confidence instead of greenbacks, there will be riches to fulfill every desire. Health prospers in an atmosphere of kindness; intelligence sharpens in an area where cooperation is the general rule; satisfaction of every human requirement resides in the community that works without competition.

Unless we realize that the role of mind (the fermenter) and the role of matter (the tractable medium) are complementary and act accordingly, we are dangerously careless. There is no worse extravagance than neglect of a great opportunity.

Let us start a campaign. Let each of us, every hour on the hour, use a fleeting half-minute to express a blessing for someone, somewhere, somehow. We can easily spare that half-minute, to elevate us as well as our target, in an infinitesimal but infinite degree.

So shall we be joining that secret society of which all members cross barriers to clasp one another heart to heart.

Are You in Love? If Not, Why Not?

It is true that the quality called love is as constant as gravity, and it is also true that we are likely to take it for granted as we take gravity. We use it and count on it and hardly trouble to value it. If we should suddenly drop a pencil and find it hanging in the air, we would be shocked by the failure of gravity. Yet often we ignore the power of love in which we move and have our being, forgetting how precious it is. It surrounds us, we lean upon it, but often we neglect to provide it for others.

Even acknowledged young lovers are often afraid to admit their mutual attraction. Sometimes the woman expects all the protestations to be voiced by the man, and the man believes that he must discipline himself to wait until the woman expresses her own desire. This occurs in various degrees, even between two who are immersed in marriage, at a time when it would be natural to suppose that they are both in a position to be generous through an innate instinct to give. Each lover would go to some trouble to select an appropriate Valentine or Christmas gift that promises devotion, and yet the confession of delicate feelings is sometimes suppressed until the ego has been placed in true perspective.

Yes, love is the means of communication most cherished, but it may be allowed to remain undeclared—or it may be used as an unfriendly test to determine who dominates. When a man introduces his lady friend to me I often say, "Oh, be kind to each other!" in a heartfelt appeal to prevent experiments with personal power.

Doubt of the other's appreciation can block the joy of showing warmth. Fear of misunderstanding, of having overrated a subtle gesture, can drown it. Willingness to allow freedom to the other may be another barrier, arising to stop the tongue when it most needs to make a declaration. Hardship in selecting the right word in a conversation can cause stuttering, and a similar difficulty can shred a loving relationship if the means of expressing it cannot be released.

Young Mrs. Starratt had been begging her husband not to raise the rent of all his senior tenants every time there was an announcement of a coming raise in Social Security benefits to counter the general inflation. She had a personal reason for being concerned, because she loved her parents and was not able to ease their difficulty when they insisted on arranging their affairs on a meager income.

Her husband merely answered, "Taxes are going up, and it's hard to find a property manager at a reasonable salary."

That gave Mrs. Starratt no satisfaction, and her love for him was one of the factors that silenced her.

While he was reading the morning paper, she watched a television presentation of a study of rewards and punishments by a psychology professor. The young speaker closed his twenty-seven minutes on the screen by telling about three little boys who entered a flower shop and seriously asked to be shown some yellow flowers. The florist gradually drew from them the information that they wanted a decoration for the funeral of their young buddy who had been hit by a truck while they were playing in the street. They proudly explained that they had taken up a collection—and had on hand exactly eighteen cents.

The florist said, "Why, I do just happen to have some yellow roses—and I can let you have them for eighteen cents . . . a dozen," and he fashioned a beautiful wreath.

Mrs. Starratt was deeply moved, and she glanced across the room at her husband who had let the newspaper fall to his knees while listening to the psychologist's talk. To her surprise she discovered that tears were rolling down the cheeks of that hardheaded businessman to whom she was married. Heretofore she had loved him, of course. But now she almost burst with a new recognition of his lovable nature. Her love for her parents and that for the little boys in the flower shop had become brackets for a new peak in her life, centering upon her husband.

(Someone asks, "Did Mr. Starratt improve his business procedure after that?" Oh, no But let us hope that in time his wife's love helped to mellow him.)

The love that outlines the pattern of society must be allowed to appear in both ideas and deeds, must add joy to an occasion or to a troubled moment. If the main object of living is to obtain happiness, then the giving of love to others is the prevailing method of crystallizing that happiness. This is not an individual matter — it is the fabric of the universe, as portrayed in the reciprocity of the whirling planets. It is the coordination of the elements, a gigantic example for human beings to follow.

What we call the omnipresence of God (in the smooth workings of creation) naturally inspires our wonder, even awe. It is the reason for the omnipotence we have seen in the attraction of worlds upon worlds. Within the whole each of us guesses at the vast control of a primary force, knowing it is that which unites us all. We realize that within us is the same talent for connection that prompts us to give. The all-powerful is invested in us, and this we are eager to nourish. Each of us wants the satisfaction of a return of what we yearn to give, but now and then we feel restraint, as though we may not be worthy.

The practical label we give the concept of God is love. Even Arnold Toynbee, the English historian, in his claim that he personally does not subscribe to any established religious organization, tells us what he knows from his own invention: "Love is divine; it is the only god that we know from experience; and man should devote himself to this god without reservations, whatever the consequences may be." This by a man who claims to have made for himself a private decision!

Certainly love is the most desirable and the only all-encompassing designation for the Eternal. We can find no other way to describe the center of the universal ability to create the universe and to administer it unendingly. We use the word *love* to explain what we consider the all-possible good for "all creatures here below."

In loneliness or other distress we cry out for this blessing, and such a cry we call a prayer. What other means of communication with a higher force do we have, after all? What other means of communication can there be for our thoughts in a structure that transcends technology? We must depend upon the spiritual passage that has no beginning and no end. Before a reach for help is formed in the human idiom, the heart has known its destination. We allow the impractical appeal to follow its secret trail, knowing intuitively that it will meet its response as soon as our thoughts are directed upon it. It is our call for love, and all that love entails is always available when we do call. Before we mention it, the heart has opened for its fast-coming answer.

Our way of accepting the love we crave is to name our need for it, our wish for it. The mere focus of the mind upon it rewards us with its blossoming in our life, for it has already been implanted in us. Nothing delays it except our acceptance of its absence. Merely knowing that we lack it draws it to us, for it has been waiting to be named, and in missing it we have already made our demand. We draw it to us when we have become ready to shelter it.

Thus, in order to keep within the area of love, we define it in whichever way our readiness allows. The first inkling prepares us to receive it, prepares us also to pass it along to others, for it is an overflowing stream always curling around obstructions and seeking to refresh with its abundance. In fact, love is a throbbing pulse, enhancing all activity and motivation, all dreams and tasks, seeking new outlets for its giving, its swelling and shining in every imaginable facet. Without it there would be no expansion, and without our generous spreading of it to others there can be only drought.

There has been plenty of attention given to Theodore Roosevelt's colorful career, and indeed he has been praised for several factors of the strenuous life. But I wonder how many have realized the fount of his power, the source of his magnetism, and the reason for his steady advance. There is one phase that has been given little publicity: his brimming over with care for others.

During the Spanish-American War, before the opening of this century, Teddy Roosevelt commanded a cavalry regiment in Cuba, since known as the Rough Riders. In that rather short campaign he had to make as good use as possible of the courageous men who served under him. At the close of hostilities the yellow fever attacked his company, and one of his most useful assistants was a man named Benjamin Franklin Daniels, who carried out his orders meticulously even though he himself was a victim of the disease. In Roosevelt's judgment this man represented love, and all the rest of his life he remembered.

When Roosevelt became president of the United States he was in a position to show his gratitude, and he appointed Ben Daniels as

U.S. marshal in Arizona. This was an appointment that had to be confirmed by the Senate, and Roosevelt gave his personal guarantee in Daniels' favor. Shortly afterward it was revealed that Ben Daniels in his youth had served a short term in a penitentiary because he had been involved with a gang of cattle rustlers. He had been released with time off for good behavior and had since then operated as an outstanding citizen, but there was the glaring blot on his career.

President Roosevelt, upon being apprised of this, was forced to ask for Ben's resignation. It was a heartbreaking situation for him as well as for Ben, because his staunch recommendation had hurt his own reputation. Personally, also, he was hurt that Ben had not disclosed the incident earlier. Nevertheless, he showed deep sorrow for Ben's feelings. He wrote one of his eloquent letters appealing to Ben not to weaken under this hardship but to live through the disappointment nobly enough to win the admiration of both his sponsors and his enemies.

Moreover, President Roosevelt communicated with the governor of Arizona and requested that Ben be named superintendent of the penitentiary in which he had been detained (a job for which no senatorial confirmation was required). In this case the governor may have required several reminders, but we have no contemporary correspondence in proof of that. It was more than two years before that superintendency became vacant, and then the governor did appoint Ben. In the meantime Ben had of course shown his capacity in other positions, but this opportunity to rise above the unsavory past was the finest gift Roosevelt could have bestowed upon him.

Not only that, but Roosevelt continued to be grateful for Ben's good qualities. In future years another opportunity for Ben's original appointment was repeated. In this instance Roosevelt wrote a detailed letter to the senators, once more requesting their confirmation of the same man to the same position as marshal. In the letter he explained the whole situation and made his request once again, upon his personal recommendation, as a token that a man might be allowed to live down a youthful mistake. Ben Daniels assumed the position earlier denied him, but the senators did not confirm him until he had been serving in that office for nine months. At last he was thoroughly vindicated, and the President too savored his own success in that regard.

In human experience there are numerous phases of love. It is love that instructs us to extend beneficence, to design harmony that in its turn enriches, invents, enlivens—and even converts new processes for its increase. Love is the high principle that leads from praise to power. It can start in a small way but it gradually widens the human possibilities. It illumines everything that it encircles, in its smallest fraction disclosing a spiritual aspect.

We reflect the gleaming reality of love's light. Each of us, seeing it from a separate viewpoint, is governed by its lessons. Nothing causes a sweeter smile than a reminiscence of a fleeting moment of love. It has long been known that love provides physical strength for individuals who meet contingencies. Many instances have been reported of an unlikely exhibition of strength for the sake of a loved one. One woman admitted that when she was too tired to see a certain job to its culmination, a phone call from a distant lover imbued her with the will to resume. It is an old tradition that a man well loved reaches unguessed heights.

Encountering love wherever we go, we find it inherent in every person, in every thing, and in every event. People we hardly know may be overflowing with it, and it enters our domain. The laughter of a child or the sigh of a passing stranger has a quickening effect.

Separately we are permeated with love, even when we fail to admit it out of modesty or out of fear that we may be accused of ulterior motive. Who are we to dare to assume that we are the expression of this tremendous force? Who are we to expect someone to respond as we wish? Of course, to be in love without return is embarrassing. Is it not wiser to conceal the dynamics of love and stay within the shield of a pretended indifference? Shall we let anyone know how vulnerable we are? Better, perhaps, to wear a mask than to indulge in confession that may invite ridicule or, worse still, pity.

Well, merely to harbor love, no matter how sternly we withhold it from view, is to float in melody, because it reemphasizes life itself. We are touching, if only by the fingertips, a layer of happiness that makes us radiate, and this alone attracts to us others who also are daring to involve themselves in love.

In fact, everywhere we turn we encounter another love story, and each one is unique. Coming to mind now is a passage in one of Anne Morrow Lindbergh's books. On an afternoon when she needed a bit of rest, she left her husband with their little son who was then three or four years old. When she returned to them an hour later she discovered that Charles Lindbergh, a man whose practical knowledge would seem miraculous to many of us and who had discoursed with men and women of various calibers, had spent this time alone with his son to present him with an unusual experience. The child was chanting:

> A bunch of the boys were whooping it
>   up in the Malamute saloon,
> The kid that handles the music box was
>   hitting a ragtime tune . . . .

Can't you imagine that child reaching a new stage of knowledge because of the tutoring of this extraordinary man? Surely the child was delighted at his momentary promotion over what he had been earlier in the day. And what, except love, could have brought about this gigantic contribution in such a short time? A father's love had respected the child's willingness to learn and had used the jollity of Bob Service's famous rhyme to create an unforgettable climax.

You see how thoroughly we are surrounded by evidences of love.

Frankly, there is no possibility that we shall ever be able to stifle it. It is continual within us and without us. It is a force as ubiquitous as gravity, as steady as a beam of light. It is an eternal consciousness that doesn't even show the result of a timid denial. It is for always, at all times, in all places, and its benefits are everlastingly spread widely. The catch is that each of us must train the eye to see, the heart to respond, the brain to accept it, and the personality to make it blossom with new sprigs. There is no escape despite our delay in believing in it.

Recognize only that you are in love as love is in you, that love is the originator of the universe because it actually is the God we so hazily try to define. It joins us with one another, attracts us to further and further goals, penetrates us with comfort. We are helpless to rebel, for it draws us to others who are in love. We must surrender, for only in love is our sustenance.

Humanity on the March

It is pleasant to notice that modern men and women are beginning to appreciate our garden, the Earth. Today we are taking practical steps to protect it from careless destruction, and this shows a new development in our understanding.

No doubt you remember the poem children used to recite: "Great, wide, beautiful, wonderful world/With the wonderful water around you curled/ . . . World, you are beautifully dressed." The closing lines of that poem must have been designed to bolster the ego of any child, for here are the words: "You are more than the Earth though you are such a dot/You can love and think, and the Earth cannot."

In that era very few of us guessed that this was an example of slander, for it was not generally recognized that the Earth was bursting with life enough and love enough to enable a myriad of creatures to flourish. Long indeed we were blind to the wealth of the mountains, prairies, rivers, oceans, the nurturing of the soil, and the richness of the rocks.

In "The Personality of Rocks," C. W. Leadbeater and Fritz Kunz have described the emotional response they found in cliffs and caves, and after quoting from their book, Dora van Gelder commented, "The Earth on which we live is peopled with these delightful, charming, and joyous beings, and so we are surrounded by everything that thrills with a sense of being alive."

Because we used to condemn as merely inert matter all that did not resemble us, we failed to guess at the separate and combining purposes of the various elements. But now, as the psychologist would say, "The being that is humanity is becoming self-conscious."

Actually, we are becoming more and more

aware of the whirling realities in space, but the little human cipher can scarcely do more than observe, even while drawing sustenance from the whole. For ages we were satisfied with our constant self-discovery, never noticing the gigantic power that had generated us. We hardly knew our own value, much less that upon which we subsisted.

Personally I regret the thousands of acres of the Earth that are at present covered with blacktop, muffling the urgent growth of the greenery that feeds living creatures. Whenever there is discussion about the hungry people on various continents I wonder why we don't get rid of the pavement that stifles vast sections of the breathing fields. (Yet many a blade of grass does emerge through asphalt slabs in its search for freedom.) We harness the weight of water for our ephemeral purposes and squander the sun's sovereignty while yet we crave its healing services.

And is anything more shameful than the way we fling poisonous waste into lakes, rivers, and coastal areas? Let us blush at the slaughter of marine life that has supplied food for our breed, aside from its numerous interconnections. Jacques Yves Cousteau, in bemoaning our treatment of this "only water planet," explains that the "expiring sea, scummed with sludge, one enormous cesspool," will (among other dangers) eliminate the oxygen essential to human breath. Not only hunger, then, but also suffocation imperils us.

Well, the human race is beginning to mature, and now we are learning to be less the enemies of life. Age is showing its worth. You may remember that the woman called George Sand, while composing her one hundred books, realized the benefits of time:

By the proper use of experience and thought one can draw much from the self. . . . It is quite wrong to think of old age as a downward slope. On the contrary, one climbs higher with the advancing years, and that, too, with surprising strides. Brainwork comes as easily to the old as physical exertion to a child. One is moving, it is true, toward the end of this life, but that end is now a goal, and not a reef on which the vessel may be dashed.

Of course, to have touched upon this theme she was already above average. Still, even her view is the least of possible visions. Compare the eternity of the worlds with our failure to surmise their substance while we long accepted the name of "mortals" though we knew better. With barely a suspicion of the whole system's invitation to advance, just the same we are trying to satisfy our needs despite our ignorance about our potential. At each "moment of time" we contrive to meet specific problems, but so far we have not suspected overall existence itself, despite our groping instinct.

Of course each of us since childhood has been showing certain talents. Regardless of their short stature, these talents have slightly contributed to the general welfare. Fortunately they constantly develop as we face larger and larger challenges. Yes, we skirmish against each new situation and so are led to more solid solutions. That is to say, the possibility of each day meets that day's emergency, but for the day following there must always be a deeper intuition to face arising perplexities.

A poet once sang, "The only things that I regret/Are the things I left undone," and it is only human to deplore our delay in learning that the universe itself is alive and thus deserves to be cherished. We really need sharper faculties, and heaven's bountiful cupboard may some day fill such an order. Until then we can only be glad to expand as rapidly as we do. We could never have been born at all if there had not been a vague prediction of possible fulfillment, and the plunge of the cosmos (so far as we know something about it) presages continually greater magnificence.

Let's not feel guilty about our past failure to perceive. We are slowly but surely progressing. I was thinking yesterday about Thomas Merton's confession of his youthful arrogance: he had prayed that his amateur manuscripts might be published "to the glory of God." Later he was embarrassed to recall this absurd audacity: how could such poor work have added to the purpose of God? And yet he was right to ask for the best he knew. As a matter of fact, after he had trained as a Trappist monk, eloquence was definitely required of him, and he was able to comply. The number of his readers who have benefited from his printed words by this time can never be approximated. Therefore, we see that his youthful struggle was toward a goal, although that goal seemed at first to be only a groundless assumption.

Each of us will improve as we make use of our opportunities. The fountain toward which our thirst strains has always been hurling its refreshment to entice us. Both the eye that sees and the feeling heart must join before advantages can crystallize. The aim for a better future strengthens the will, and through the will the wisdom that we slowly acquire turns into a further purpose. There is a universal drive to become better, and we are all stirred by every next possibility, surrounded by more than we deserve because there is infinitely more than we can imagine. Daily happenings arouse a craving for the still unseen. The mind has a mystical conviction that more can yet be found, and each of us prepares for a new joy that might long ago have been ours had we only known how to accept it. Each day we reflect a wider horizon than yesterday's. If this growth does no more than cause us to cast a kindly eye upon a neighbor, that generous appraisal may win a smile of friendship which, in turn, may nourish a bud of lovingness. Thus the slow unfolding takes place.

Sir Alister Hardy asks, "Is love the force that has always been animating the organic world?"

Why not? Perhaps the universal love we have hardly dared to count upon is the true center of our consciousness. Have we ignored this because we tried to separate the objective from the subjective in our zeal to purge the personal?

Does not the same force that swings both the small and the mighty operate through humanity? Whatever has established the sun's energy may very well be the same fuel that excites the human senses. You know that scientists once claimed evolution as an entirely physical stream. Why have we so long neglected to see that what we call natural is close to what we call supernatural? If God is not natural, what is?

All the productive activity that we can trace has come from the invisible, so why draw the shade against whatever is not concrete? We have patronizingly implied that what we call God must lie beyond the sense realm—but why? Why could It not be accessible through ordinary channels?

In studying biology we observe its details and reactions, allying it with chemistry. Of late we have seen that this study responds to mental efforts (even to visceral control). But why have we not until now analyzed the rudiments of memory, the measure of conscience, the purport of sorrow and delight? It sometimes seems that whatever makes living precious has been shelved instead of being investigated. Until we find a paved path toward the study of intangibles we make excuses to forget them.

Those who seem to know have declared

that love is the greatest force exerted. It has been suppressed among humans even in the field of religion, but there has never been any cessation of our effort to define a holy layer. No intellectual exercise has ever overtaken our yearning toward our Source, but seldom do we try to estimate our rapture. Before us still lies the task to engage in a more subtle form of research.

John Langdon Davies is quoted as saying:

The whole history of science has been a direct search for God . . . Copernicus, Kepler, Galileo, Newton, Leibniz, and the rest did not merely believe in God in an orthodox way; they believed that their work told humanity more about God than had been known before. . . . They regarded their discoveries not only as proving God's existence, but as revealing more and more of His nature.

Until recently warfare, for instance, though admitted to be an evil, has been accepted as something to be endured because of its result in good (for the winner). At last we frame a new question: Is there any logic in war?

What has delayed us in asking this obvious question? What slow reversion has finally arrived at a faint awakening to the idea that perhaps the answer is already clear. By what means shall we now redeem the race from brutality?

Because there is no longer the illusion of profit from contest, an international disavowal of war as a means of settling disputes has become emphatic. Attempts to construct peace among us will lead to success only when there is the conglomerate heart's hunger for peace. In order to avoid annihilation of the Earth and all its inhabitants we shall have to create a better custom than competition.

The stimulating luster of the next stage of civilization entices us. Because barbarism is too dangerous to be allowed to continue, we must stoutly turn against it. Our only safety is cooperation among nations as among neighbors. That irresistible charm draws our aspiration, and now even selfish souls yearn to catch its gleam.

Acknowledge it now: man in separate strife is in danger, and our garden, the Earth, will die if we revert to wholesale barbarism. Only in the climate of charity can we appoint a decent goal for us and our planet. Love is the consolation that we crave, and foresight is our assurance that we shall at last uncover it. Our destiny, whether we can foresee it or not, is already on the drawing board. Success for more than the human family is assured as soon as we catch up with it.

Let us dare to ask for utmost enlightenment. When we produce cooperation we shall have the secret. The human animal, in whose hands the future of the whole world rests, is a clever builder when he knows what he must build.

What Is Your Intention?

It was a pleasure recently to open a book by Rollo May and find him saying, "We are living at a time when one age is dying and the new age is not yet born." That is an excellent prospect, for change can make way for progress. Of course someone may object that things may get worse. Well, that depends on your intention.

How well Rollo May understands this! He continues: "A choice confronts us. Shall we, as we feel our foundations shaking, become paralyzed and cover our inaction with apathy? Then we will have surrendered our chance to participate in the forming of the future."

And he explains that the distinctive characteristic of a human being is the talent to influence through awareness. How exciting!

During the past hundred years the public has been gradually persuaded that it is possible to rise above the low ceiling of materialism. The quality of the twentieth century, it seems to me, is the courage of the populace to march in a phalanx toward broader vistas.

This is a noticeable contrast with previous historical periods. There used to be only one courageous leader at a time, traveling alone (like Francis Bacon, for instance), and declaring that an unbelievably daring task could be accomplished whenever the full human potential should be tapped. The average person never accepted such an idea until enough time had passed to arouse enough followers (by ones and twos) to give it status. Until then it was the custom among the majority to smile condescendingly at the solitary thinker and his cheerful promise.

A rare individual may have been heard to say that one gravitates toward what one thinks about. Next it was rumored that if you want a thing, you must think of it steadily, and you will get it. But even then we were far from guessing that the mind could take the initiative in acquiring what we wanted.

Now we have learned that a definite intention helps us to advance. Frances Foulks says "to become a mighty magnet to receive the good" we must incite "the true power of concentration, which is interest and attention to the one thing that one desires to do or be." It is the intention that supplies the incentive to outline a purpose, and purpose molds a goal to improve the mode of living.

Yes, that realization has been long in coming to the general public. Once an old-fashioned lethargy permitted complaints about "bad luck" to be accepted. Today we are bombarded by conceptions that quicken the dullest of us to take a higher aim. Many inventive minds are publishing inspiring books to invest us with a positive sense. Besides, the calendar is filled with conventions at which innovators describe their aspirations to large professional audiences. The consensus is that nothing could better jolt the listeners out of their favorite ruts. The generous exchange of philosophical and scientific discoveries promotes a fellowship that must go down in the record as proof that civilization has arrived.

One of these events was the First National Congress for Integrative Health at Tucson, sponsored by the Academy of Parapsychology and Medicine. One of the speakers was Willis Harman, a Stanford University professor and director of the Center for the Study of Social Policy.

Dr. Harman assured the assemblage that science and spirit are the two keys to our destiny: science as the outward-looking approach, spirit as the inward-turning religious aspect. He explained that lack of balance between these two has led to the current quandary about health care—or, rather, "sickness care," as it is called by a leading insurance official.

We now find it necessary to alter mental habits in order to avoid the anxieties that resulted from cultural dictates of a past era.

What was satisfactory in 1880 is not satisfactory today, and we are exploring other avenues than those that previously seemed adequate. Of course the dilemma is itself a means of transition; we know that something better may be found just around the corner—even though it may not yet be defined.

During the Fifties the writer Henry Miller observed many young people groping for a solution to their discontent, and during the Seventies there was another generation making the same pilgrimage away from the stereotype that crippled their elders.

Well, there are still many such wanderers, most of them truly seeking the ideal because they refuse to settle down in a situation now seen to be an absurd imposition. They are willing (eager) to work, but not in a *cul-de-sac*. They prefer to suffer cold and hunger and snubs and their parents' disappointment rather than subscribe to the "respectable" routine that they discount.

One young adventurer said to me, "Sometimes I almost thought I'd have to surrender," but he continued to defy failure by feeding on the nutritive grasses and herbs he knew how to find in the fields. At last he fitted snugly into the sort of program that he knew could develop his peculiar talents.

Dr. Harman too has witnessed such youthful attempts to forge a dramatic social change while denying "a world they never made." He knows that many of us have already sustained lasting scars from such efforts, and others have fallen into poor health when finding no satisfaction. Therefore we must create a method that chimes with the new implications, and members of the medical profession are feeling the pressure to produce a more pliable means of curing the restless.

Increased crime is the defiant answer of those who see no purpose in life. Helpless in the face of government laxity, hopeless before the deterioration of organized religion, comfortless when lacking direction, the wasteful ones fling themselves into destruction without any recognition of responsibility. For a long time each such glaring fault was labeled as separate from the others but, truth to tell, they are all related. Without a solution people are swept by a gigantic tide further and further away from a view of the lighthouse.

The so-called official truth provides no guidance, and establishment power has no justification. Intellectual abilities alone are unable to resolve problems that they themselves have inaugurated, for in serving technology they cater to industry. Until these two are rededicated to the advancement of human development, the masses will continue to suffer. They are striving for productive roles to play—they want to "go somewhere worth going to," Dr. Harman reminded us.

Friend Endicott is a six-footer whose normal weight is two hundred and who is famous in his field. While his wife was ill he teetered from hope to despair, and when she died he was assailed with loneliness, halfway believing he could not live without her. Suddenly he learned that shortly before her death his wife, without his knowledge, had signed over to a relative her half of the joint tenancy of their home.

Endicott reacted to the shock by falling into the old, childish "Then I won't play!" as though under such circumstances life would not be worth living. To everybody's surprise, he became paralyzed from the waist down. He could not stand, much less walk, and subconsciously he thought the solution to everything would be his quick death. For some months he remained in bed while friends served him as well as they could, and he became puzzled as to why he was not able merely to die and be through with the whole problem. He was stronger than he had suspected. Outwardly he wanted to get well, but silently he continued to hold tight to the unconscious death wish.

When all this was made clear to him, as he lay in bed he suddenly raised both knees — the first time they had been called upon to act naturally since his surrender to the shock.

That was only yesterday, but I firmly expect that the next time I call on him he will bound to the door to greet me with a hug. For a man of his stature nothing less is possible.

Bewilderment and self-doubt always interfere with normal health, and modern biofeedback at times gives an opportunity to do something about it. This new method of examining and measuring what is going on inside the body at least occupies attention — and it often enables the distressed person to stabilize his faculties.

Until now inner thought has been accused of containing no reality. But when some ideas are automatically suppressed they erupt into disease of one kind or another, demanding the listening ear. Little by little we are acknowledging that the silence within has value. Even the old battle of science against religion is winding down. Indeed, the entire area of human experience is causing a wholesale alteration in the very metaphors of science.

At last it is clear that change is not devastating but actually gratifying, especially when the fund of scientific knowledge is no longer restricted to the mechanistic. Rather, the framework of a desirable future entices us away from traditional dead ends, and instinctively we enlarge upon our hidden potential by fashioning motivation. More and more we admit that creative thinking is part of our natural equipment, and we listen to our hunches. This is the way we have found "an invisible and subtle science in the spirit of the whole universe."

To quote the Upanishads, said Dr. Harman, "Thou art that," so we stop denying the inner conviction. We also stop fearing the god-life within us, as Abraham Maslow expressed it, and we set up a motive for our actions. Then our "authority of progress through the alignment of choices" becomes our pilot. "We assume the privilege of bringing into existence the patterns of the divine Architect."

The power of suggestion, stronger than we have assumed it to be, reveals the great secret: "I am the cause." All I suffer is of my personal design, and all I win is of my personal determination. In every circumstance I am the arbiter of my destiny. This establishes the I-am-godlike attitude, the non-attached impersonality.

Dr. Harman quoted Emerson in saying,

"Love must become more impersonal every day" (and, indeed, it is scarcely love until it has become impersonal).

Inasmuch as health is the responsibility of each of us, we must claim our wholeness and live up to the challenge. It is said that there is only one disease (a bad self-image) and only one social ill (an unwholesome image of man's place in the universe). The true perspective can correct both evils.

Throughout history, philosophy and religion have been creative forces in society. In the past, however, discoveries by the few have often been buried by the disbelief of the many. But now the mass of experience is not the property of any single group—it accumulates into the living heritage of mankind. Therefore the populace benefits, and no regression is excusable. Materialism has been endured at great cost, but now it is superannuated. Let it go! Rollo May says, "To live into the future means to leap into the unknown, and this requires a degree of courage for which there is no immediate precedent and which few people realize."

The longer I live, the more meaning I see in this old quotation from "The Cloud of Unknowing": "Forasmuch as thou willest it and desirest it, so much hast thou of it, and no more nor no less."

Since it is true that we have only what we think we have, let's polish up our intention and travel straight toward it. We have the enterprise, and we shall make the future what we want it to be.

The Best Is Yet to Come!

Shakespeare asks, "What is the end of study?" and in one sense there is no end. Out of silence the waves of communication move upon us from all sides without cessation, and we are always learning, while "the world is upswung into being."

In another sense *end* means *purpose,* and purpose never becomes a finality but always remains a reason to persist. There is no stoppage, never a point from where there can be no further enticement.

These days there is great talk about ecology as though it were a new discovery and a means of merely obtaining practical supplies. But long ago the Irish mystic, George William Russell, realized that "gradually the earth lover realizes the golden world is all about him in imperishable beauty, and he may pass from the vision to the profounder beauty of being, and know an eternal love is within and around him, pressing upon him and sustaining with infinite tenderness his body, his soul, and his spirit."

The wealth of the earth nourishes all that we are, especially the fundamental inner layer that supports the outer in all its phases. Every moment is only another seed to encourage renewed growth, every perception another promise that further understanding must evolve.

I remember waking one clear, cold, pine-scented morning at dawn and feeling the luxury of the straight ground beneath my sleeping bag as my eyes opened to the green lace of the Sequoia foliage far above me. Nearby, the stimulating dash of the Kings River foamed over rocks and fallen tree trunks. Oh, the glory, the privacy, in this cradle of health and vigor! It was beyond anything I had hoped for and seemed to be the ultimate culmination. If only I could halt here, I thought, and savor this felicity forever!

I almost pleaded with the friend who was conducting this safari, "Do let us spend our whole vacation here." But I spoke no such entreaty, for intuitively I realized that our leader's experience contained wisdom not yet open to my view.

And then, as we climbed higher in the Sierra Nevada, each scene, each fragrance, each tumbling stream, and the fantasia of sunshine became an increasing splendor. I whispered to myself, "I might not have seen this!"

Above the timberline the bare granite peaks showed the grandeur of simplicity in the sheer white contours. Being without vegetation or other distraction, they sparkled with the resolution of integrity, releasing us from obligation to pretend, transcending our preconceptions. The vitality of the unspoiled earth transmuted into our personalities a portion of that which enables the universe to endure.

All this we should have missed if we had

failed to continue the journey. I instructed myself: "No matter where you may be, always remember there are farther places to be prized as well!" and I meant that to be my philosophy for the future.

This recollection frequently causes me to appreciate the hastening moments, and I can apply this attitude even to the long succession of books on modern psychology that are currently ministering to the hunger of an inquiring public. Any one of those books may please, but none alone is enough. The next and the next conducts a reader, deliberately or by inference, to the reminder that we are more than we seem to be.

Internally we have always suspected that we are fashioned in deeper dimension than a stranger can see at a glance in passing. But we have usually denied this out of modesty, in the absence of evidence that our self-esteem had basis. Now, however, because of these optimistic publications we can expand.

The barber said gravely: "I thought there'd never be another chance for me to learn. But somebody told me about a book that shows you how to live better—psycho-something."

The young woman who comes to wax my floor said: "I found out you don't have to settle for the same old thing your parents had. I read a book that says there's things we can do if we try."

A printer told me breathlessly: "I used to spend every evening after work at the pool hall, because I thought there was nothing else to do. But then I met Blanche, and she was reading books about making your life spread out. It sure is lucky I met Blanche!"

In a lecture an Italian musicologist explained: "Of course many forgotten operas were composed during the hundred years before Verdi. Without them there could never have been a Verdi."

So Verdi's talent had fed on the work of his predecessors while he strove to extend the truth of himself. Those lost composers, when facing worldly failure, may have felt they had wasted their time, but they were paving the way. Many steps lead to the heights, and all the books we read today rightly engage us to live more courageously as we too aim to fulfill our own destinies.

I have heard about an Oriental man who introduced himself by saying, "My miserable superstition is Buddhism—what is yours?"

He was warning the new acquaintance of the bias by which he would hear the conversation and by which his answers would be shaped. In return he wanted to know the bias by which his new acquaintance would speak, so that he could decode the language as he listened, for he had every intention of bridging the gap.

You may already have noticed that it is much easier to talk from a definite standpoint, especially on a controversial subject. When a Christian speaks of Jesus, in that one word he conveys the tradition of the last two thousand years. But this facility is denied the Muhammadan, who in his turn relies upon a quite different shortcut. He can transmit his idea to a colleague in a few words, but in speaking with the Christian he must use circuitous explanations.

And today we notice that, for a psychologist's assertions to carry weight, there must be a whole new technique of communication. There is so far no basic code to imply an inherited pattern, and laboratory jargon has not yet been polished to an art. But for centuries the word *prayer* has had a universal acceptance, so here I feel comfortable in using that term as I speak about personal euphoria.

The first active exercise for extracting benefit from constructive reading about abstract values may very well be by means of a conventional prayer learned in the preconscious years. No matter how formal it sounds, it does expend its share of force to cause reaction in the mind. A prayer, whether it be a pitiful complaint, a personal petition, or a cry of thanksgiving, elicits a physiological, or a psychological, or a social result. It assuredly shoots at a target, and the aspiration is a remedy in itself.

As a replacement for passivity, prayer makes room for a new factor, signifying a willingness to correct character traits. It is primarily an investment in dedication, and the undeniable consequence carries gratification.

If we pray for clarification to solve a problem, the troublesome knot unravels. If we pray for improved health, a new habit of taking care of the body inserts itself into the general program with such a natural result that we say, "It would have happened anyway." If we pray for the soothing of a human relationship, an uninvited component of pleasure appears as though it had always been there.

Perplexed as we are in an incomprehensible cosmos, we attempt to surpass what we are at any given moment, so we plug our prayer into our highest concept of God. It cannot fail to extend the consciousness, even though at first it merely breaks through the wall of the "dark little human brain."

After our first experimental period with prayer has left an impression, our attention is focused upon what earlier seemed shadowy enough to pass as the product of imagination. In reluctant wonder, now we seriously assume a veritable experience beyond mere recital of doctrine. That is why we respond to the modern psychology books with a whisper, "Something better than we guessed is true, is true!"

Bertrand Russell was familiar with this reaction, for he wrote: "The first and most direct outcome of the illumination is belief in the possibility of a way of knowledge which may be called revelation or insight or intuition, as contrasted with sense, reason, and analysis. Closely connected with this belief is the conception of a Reality behind the world of appearance and utterly different from it."

It may be said that even in the selection of our reading material we are led by subconscious inclination from one clue to another, for while we are still full of doubt we accept as the central fact of existence that we are susceptible to Authority. For this very reason we welcome new possibilities and try to enlarge our awareness.

As we move slowly into improved consciousness, we reflect that what has seemed until now only fantasy is an honest report about the unknown. Even in such a primary stage, our personal choice combats the "downward tendency to matter." There is never any static course, because all elements are in constant motion, and therefore we choose to be propelled into a wider orbit. Only by degrees do we become persuaded that we want something that is already beckoning. Then we let the stronger tide take over.

Drifting into keener and keener perceptivity, we partake of the company of others who are converging upon the same course. Meister Heinrich Eckhart emphasized that love of God must overflow in the form of love for fellowman, and automatically this develops while the comfort of aloneness continues in the freedom to advance at our own pace.

Impelled by the dynamic impulse ("always by the process of growth," to quote Bergson), we sense the supremacy of the purified order before we meet with it. But when it floods us, the reborn personality forgets the obstacles of the past which no doubt had been devising it all along.

No longer do we look for a solution to the world's disharmonies. On the contrary, now external things seem already reconciled; all that previously seemed needful of correction has been nullified in the goal of perfection toward which it is bent. We see truths that were once invisible. The ardor of personal desire pales "when all vain love and dread, vain joy and sorrow, is cast out of the heart, so that it loves nothing but God," as Walter Hilton reminds us.

It is for the sake of this gradual ascent that we continue to read the writings of those who have preceded us. The mail carrier with five children to raise on a circumscribed wage lifted his face and said earnestly, "I'll never forget you, Mrs. Fortnut, because you showed me this book." He had found a new path to follow.

I too am grateful for every forerunner of many gentle promotions, of which an outstanding symbol is that summer of my elevation in the Sierra Nevada when the mind was forced to lean upon itself. How I regretted having to return to the lowlands! So I dallied at Mt. Rainier and Taku Glacier and Banff and Lake Louise, before letting myself down into the bustle of New York City. There, still vibrating to the scintillation of the heights, quite naturally I drifted through the museum where Nicholas Roerich's bright paintings of the Himalaya echoed my secret joy.

As Russell wrote: "The Mighty Mother is that earth whose holy substance they call common clay. The Spirit is the strength of our being, the power which binds atom to atom and earth to heaven. The Christos is the Magician of the beautiful, not only the Architect of the God-world, but it is that in us which sees beauty, creates beauty. We could not lift an eyelash but that we have our Being in Him."

Now in memory of mountains I credit each of the good influences that leads us on and on. The printing press at the moment is doing a great service in urging us to aspire. Those of you who are on a similar pilgrimage, seeing every step as a new beginning, can wholeheartedly cry to others, "*Bon voyage* and Godspeed!"

RECOMMENDED READING

Anonymous, *The Cloud of Unknowing,*
ed. Evelyn Underhill
Assagioli, Roberto, *Synthesis*
Buber, Martin, *The Way of Response*
Bucke, Richard Maurice, *Cosmic Consciousness*
Fechner, Gustave, *The Little Book of Life After Death*
Heywood, Rosalind, *Beyond the Reach of Sense*
James, William, *Varieties of Religious Experience*
Johnson, Raynor C., *The Imprisoned Splendor*
Jung, Carl Gustav, *Memories, Dreams, Reflections*
Koestler, Arthur, *Insight and Outlook;*
The Roots of Coincidence
Murchie, Guy, *The Seven Mysteries of Life*
Murphy, Gardner, *Human Potentialities*
Oyle, Irving, *The Healing Mind;*
Time, Space, and the Mind
Rhine, J. B., *The Reach of the Mind*
Rhine, Louisa, *Hidden Channels of the Mind*
Underhill, Evelyn, *Practical Mysticism*
Whitman, Walt, *Leaves of Grass*

(The titles listed above are not available for purchase through Unity Books. Send for our book list and information about the Unity Book Club, Unity Village, Mo. 64065.)

Printed U.S.A.

143-F-3390-15M-5-79